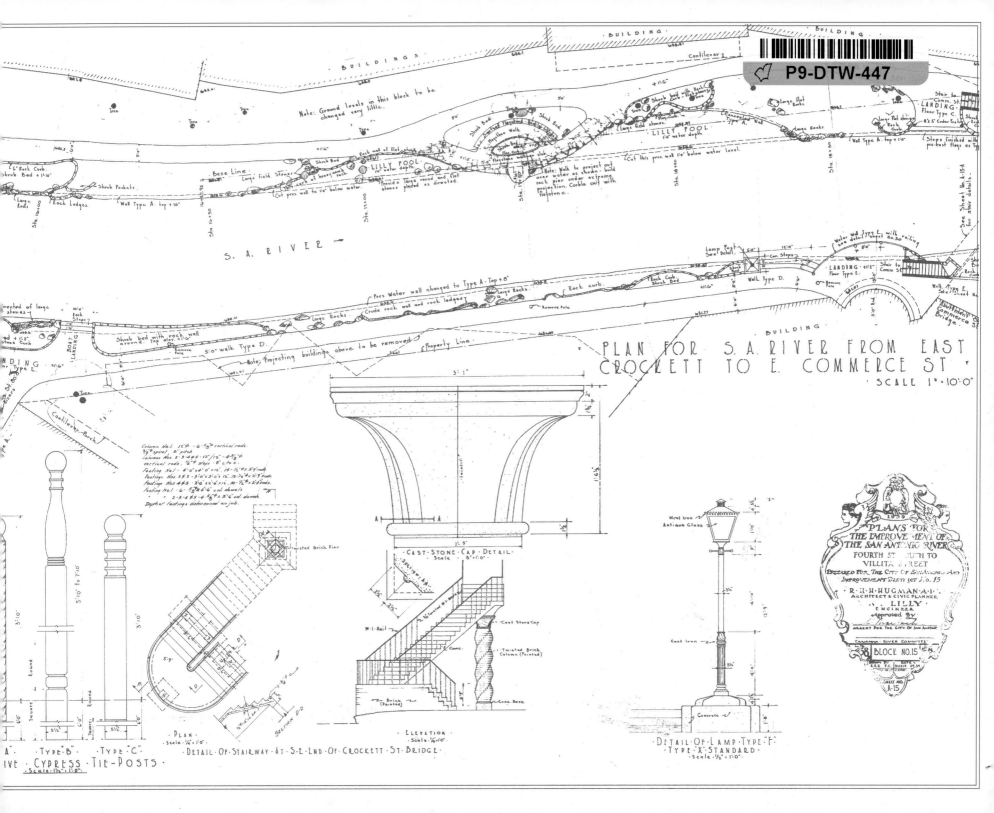

S. A. RIVER →

PLAN FOR S. A. RIVER FROM EAST CROCKETT TO E. COMMERCE ST.
SCALE 1" = 10'-0"

CAST STONE CAP DETAIL
Scale 3" = 1'-0"

ELEVATION
Scale 1/4" = 1'-0"

PLAN
Scale 1/4" = 1'-0"

DETAIL OF STAIRWAY AT S. E. END OF CROCKETT ST. BRIDGE

DETAIL OF LAMP TYPE "F"
TYPE "X" STANDARD
Scale 1/2" = 1'-0"

TYPE "B"   TYPE "C"
CYPRESS TIE-POSTS
Scale 1 1/2" = 1'-0"

PLANS FOR
THE IMPROVEMENT OF
THE SAN ANTONIO RIVER
FOURTH STREET SOUTH TO
VILLITA STREET
Prepared For The City Of San Antonio And
Improvement District No. 15
R. H. H. HUGMAN A. I.
ARCHITECT & CIVIC PLANNER
LILLY
ENGINEER
Approved By
AGENT FOR THE CITY OF SAN ANTONIO
CHAIRMAN RIVER COMMITTEE
BLOCK NO. 15
SHEET NO.
A-15

River Walk

River Walk

THE EPIC STORY
OF SAN ANTONIO'S RIVER

★

Lewis F. Fisher

"1" />

"1" />

MAVERICK PUBLISHING COMPANY

Maverick Publishing Company
P. O. Box 6355, San Antonio, Texas 78209

Library of Congress Cataloging-in-Publication Data

Fisher, Lewis F.
River Walk : the epic story of San Antonio's river / Lewis F. Fisher.
p. cm.
Includes bibliographical references and index.
ISBN-13: 978-1-893271-40-1 (hardcover, alk. paper)
ISBN-13: 978-1-893271-40-8 (softcover, alk. paper)
1. Paseo del Rio (San Antonio, Tex.)–History. 2. San Antonio (Tex.)–History.
3. San Antonio River (Tex.) – History. 4. Paseo del Rio (San Antonio, Tex.) – History – Pictorial works.
5. San Antonio (Tex.) – History – Pictorial works.
6. San Antonio River (Tex.) – History–Pictorial works. I. Title.
F394.S2117P37 2006
976.4'351--dc22
2006019866

Printed in China

13579108642

Book and jacket design by Janet Brooks / Brooks Art&Design / Austin, TX

Frontispiece: The Arneson River Theater as completed by the WPA in 1941.

Contents

San Antonio's River Walk now extends for nearly three miles through downtown San Antonio, between the northern end at Lexington Street, top, and, at bottom, Nueva Street, with walkways but no boats continuing on south into the King William Historic District.

The River Walk's heart is the original Great Bend channel, in the shape of a sideways horseshoe. A flood control cutoff channel connecting the ends of the horseshoe is now part of the River Walk, as are the extensions east of the bend into the Convention Center, lower right, and, to its north, Rivercenter Mall.

Major north-south streets within the bend and east of the cutoff channel are, from left, St. Mary's, Navarro, and Presa. East of the bend are Losoya Street and, at an angle, Alamo Street. The Alamo is in the park at center right.

Major east-west streets inside the bend are, from below from the northern leg, Crockett, Commerce, and Market. North of the bend are the three-block-long east-west College Street and, above it, Houston Street.

The building with the flowered roof on the bend's southern leg is Villita Assembly Hall, just west of the Arneson River Theater.

PREFACE

When I came to San Antonio for military training early in 1964, I was more taken with dining outdoors on Mexican food beside the San Antonio River than with the fine points of precision drill. It was still winter back home in western New York. I couldn't remember an outdoor restaurant open up there even in July. Five years later, when my San Antonio–born bride suggested that I start out as a daily newspaper reporter in her hometown, the vision of having enchiladas on the River Walk whenever I wanted helped make the decision easy.

Thirty years and many Regular Plates later, I found myself commissioned by the San Antonio Conservation Society to write the book that became *Saving San Antonio: The Precarious Preservation of a Heritage*. Everyone knew how the Conservation Society had been organized in 1924 to save the river. It was common knowledge that its members had put on a puppet show about the river that convinced a demonic city council not to drain and pave an unkempt stream, but rather to save it and adopt architect Robert Hugman's plan for the River Walk.

The developed River Walk had reached the point where it was generating $3 billion a year for San Antonio's economy. It was alternating with the Alamo as the top travel attraction in Texas, and had become a world-renowned model for sensitive river development. I set out to document how this all began.

First I looked for the Conservation Society's minutes from the late 1920s, when the turnaround was said to have occurred. Unfortunately, the secretary at the time had died while in office and her minutes were burned by her family. City council minutes? It turned out the puppet show was presented after a session adjourned, so no record there—nor could I find any recorded suggestion in the council minutes of paving over the river. Clippings? Documents? All were from later years and told variations of the long-familiar story. Curiously, early histories of the society's first decades written by its members mentioned nothing about saving the river, as they surely would have were it a pivotal factor as later claimed.

If any source was cited in later accounts, it was an article in the Conservation Society's newsletter written by the society's first president, Emily Edwards, in 1966. This despite the fact that Miss

Edwards's cover letter stated that her account "does not pretend to be a complete one," and was written "just to suggest a continuity of interest."

There was nowhere else to turn. So, with the backing of the society's book committee, I set about scanning microfilm of the San Antonio *Express*, starting in 1924 and continuing, day by day, until I found a contemporary report of the key events reported by Miss Edwards. At last I thought I had a fit—a public meeting called by the Conservation Society in 1926 at the Menger Hotel in which Judge Sidney Brooks strongly backed the society, just as Miss Edwards described in her article.

The meeting as reported, however, was called not to support the Conservation Society in saving the river, but rather to support the Daughters of the Republic of Texas in their proposed purchase of additional land around the Alamo. Judge Brooks strongly backed the proposal. Conservation Society leaders were present. But there was not a word about the San Antonio River.

So I slogged on through microfilms to the end of 1929. Nothing else came close, even though in those days such events were chronicled much more carefully than similar happenings have been in recent years. Had Miss Edwards, writing forty years later, misremembered? Or, since she was living in Mexico in the late 1920s, had she relied on recollections of others?

What did emerge in contemporary news accounts was a portrait of a preservation group organized in an unsuccessful attempt to save the city's Greek Revival market house and then incorporated to save San Antonio's crumbling eighteenth century Mission San José complex, a feat heroically accomplished.

The original script of Miss Edwards's puppet show, in her own handwriting, was found safely preserved in Conservation Society files. It did not mention the river except in passing. The script being made generally available happened to be the one she rewrote in the mid-1950s to emphasize the river's importance. Those were years when River Walk designer Robert Hugman's project, undertaken by the WPA, was neglected and in danger of being carved up. Rather than supporting Hugman, other research revealed that many of the society's leaders had conspired to have him fired midway through the project. In the mid-1950s, however, the Conservation Society did step in and, in a real sense, helped save the River Walk.

As it turned out, the section of the San Antonio River that wound through downtown was saved more than twenty years before the Conservation Society was organized. Since 1914 its banks had been preserved as a city park, authorized by a river-loving city council, not one trying to bury the river, as later portrayed. The plan to bury the river was first formally proposed—and quickly rejected—in 1911, not in 1926 or 1928 or whenever, and was never endorsed by the council. Nor were the park's banks derelict in the 1920s. They were well maintained up to the time the WPA work began, in 1938.

Amazingly, the engaging, well-told tales had turned out to be mostly fables. They had been woven so tightly into the River Walk information distributed that they threw virtually all local, state, and national writers on the subject far off track. The longer the telling of the River Walk's background prior to 1938, the more hopelessly garbled the account became.

To my relief, the San Antonio Conservation Society took it all rather well. Copies of the original script of the puppet show—a remarkable presentation even still—replaced copies of the later one in society press kits. News releases and background materials were appropriately adjusted. But long-cherished myths die hard, and other sources seemed a bit reluctant to adjust to the new reality. We can expect to hear the myths again, even from those who should know better.

While in the tedious process of scanning microfilms, I also happened to piece together an account of the tumultuous 1920s flood control efforts that made the River Walk possible. After completing *Saving San Antonio*, I did additional research unrelated to that book and in 1997 wrapped it up in *Crown Jewel of Texas*.

After the book's publication, more long-buried information kept surfacing. Seven years of trolling eBay and keeping a watchful eye on other sources of vintage images have reaped a far broader visual story of the river park and the River Walk than that available for *Crown Jewel*. Too, the River Walk itself has kept evolving.

By the time the second printing of *Crown Jewel* sold out, it was obvious that an entirely new work was needed. This, at last, is that book.

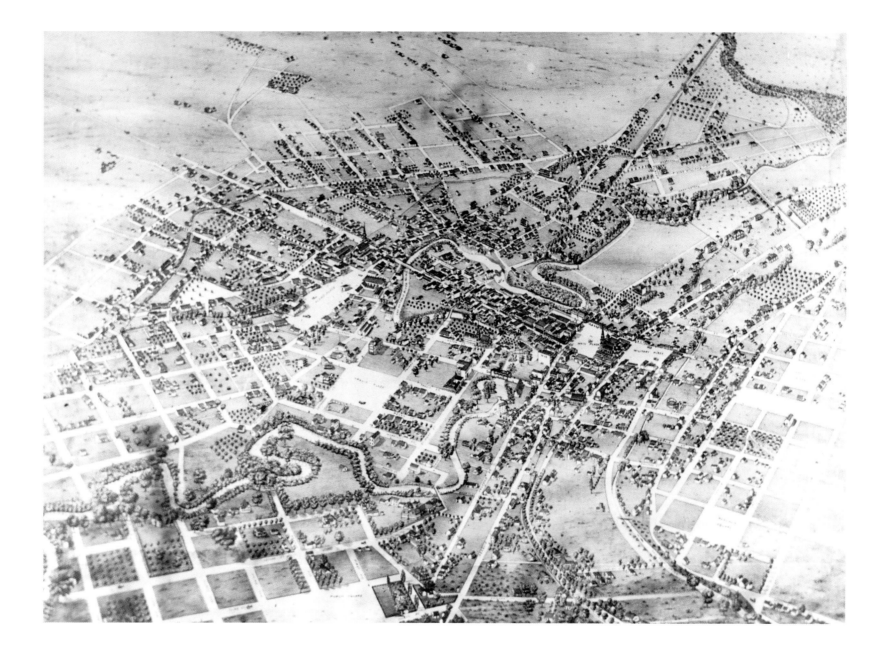

1
SAN ANTONIO'S RIVER

San Antonio's narrow river gave its first settlers no clue that it would ever be more than simply a source of water. It lacked the volume and slope to power anything bigger than small mills, so there was no big industry in its future. It was not navigable to the sea, so San Antonio could hardly become a Texas port city—nor was there ever a significant town at the river's mouth, 180 miles to the southeast on the Gulf of Mexico.

The lush springs at the river's headwaters near San Antonio could, however, provide an oasis of sorts on the far frontier of New Spain, nourishing a colorful community for more than a century and a half until growth exceeded the river's ability to support it. Like seaports, inland San Antonio managed to gain its own amalgam of foreign tongues and cultures early on. Cowboys and trail drivers mingled with natives and a host of immigrants newly arrived from Europe. Central plazas became points of arrival and embarkation for travelers and wagon trains. In the eighteenth century, convoys lumbered to and from Spanish missions on the frontier with French Louisiana and, in the next century, to and from distant places on the western frontier of Texas and in northern Mexico.

In the 1850s nearly half of all San Antonians were foreign-born, and the dominant language was German. When Frederick Law Olmsted, the landscape architect about to design New York City's Central Park, passed through in 1856, he famously wrote of San Antonio's "jumble of races, costumes, languages, and buildings," which, he noted, lent San Antonio an "odd and antiquated foreignness."[1]

But after the railroad finally arrived in 1877, the sudden growth that followed could no longer be sup-

opposite page
The river winds lazily through San Antonio in this 1873 bird's eye view looking southeast. At the center, the Great Bend, now the heart of the River Walk, curves sharply to the left, then sharply right and then sharply right again to flow around the peninsula then known as Bowen's Island and since eliminated by the river's straightening. Also gone is the large bend toward lower left, now the site of Municipal Auditorium.

left
Wagon trains drawn by oxen head down Commerce Street in 1870s San Antonio, noted for its "odd and antiquated foreignness."

ported by overburdened spring-fed streams. New water required from artesian wells lowered the water table to the point that headwaters springs began to disappear. During droughts the river's flow disappeared altogether, and the river seemed doomed to extinction.

An unsightly, barren riverbed did not please San Antonians, for they were accustomed to hearing lyrical praise for the stream. "Rich blue and as pure as crystal," Olmsted had observed. "One could lean for hours over the bridge rail."

"A lovely milky-green," thought Sidney Lanier a few decades later, as he waxed on about "winding vistas of sweet lawns running down to the water, of weeping willows kissing its surface, . . . combing the long sea-green locks of a trailing watergrass which sends its waving tresses down the center of the current."[2]

San Antonians delighted in the confusion of visitors who crossed bridges—two dozen bridges by the end of the nineteenth century—wondering each time if they were crossing a different stream. "You cannot escape it," marveled one visitor of the river. "You think you have left it behind you, and there it is before you."[3] The river seemed to fit the laid-back ambience of the town, wandering thirteen miles to reach a point only six miles distant.

In 1691 the river was named San Antonio for St. Anthony, whose statue, given to the city by Portugal at the time of HemisFair '68, stands beside the extended River Walk.

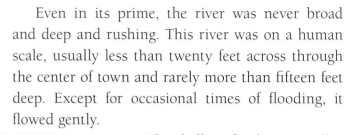

Even in its prime, the river was never broad and deep and rushing. This river was on a human scale, usually less than twenty feet across through the center of town and rarely more than fifteen feet deep. Except for occasional times of flooding, it flowed gently.

The shallow, fertile river valley charmed the cluster of soldiers and priests under Domingo Terán de los Ríos and Father Damian Massanet in 1691 as they traveled to the struggling Spanish missions of East Texas. The spring-fed headwaters of two streams—the river and, two miles to the west, a tributary creek—happened to be on the southern edge of an upthrust known as the Balcones Escarpment. The spring waters, freed from the overbearing rock of the escarpment and forced upward by pressure of water below, sent the river and San Pedro Creek meandering lazily, as water does on land with little slope.

It was June 13, the day of St. Anthony of Padua. Thus the Spaniards named the spot—which the Indians called Yanaguana—San Antonio de Padua. The group then moved on to the Louisiana frontier, where the French were stirring up the Indians and casting longing eyes on Spanish silver mines in northern Mexico across the nearly empty land between.

The East Texas missions needed a way station closer than the nearest Spanish settlements at the time, far away on the Rio Grande. Two decades later, planners remembered the verdant site a third of the way toward East Texas. So it was that the founders of San Antonio arrived on May 1, 1718. A few Spanish soldiers under Governor Martín de Alarcón threw together a presidio, and some Franciscan priests under Father Antonio de San Buenaventura y Olivares established Mission San Antonio de Valero.

The founders chose not to set up on the densely wooded and boggy terrain surrounding the river's headwaters, where the largest of dozens of springs rose through a crevice in the gray limestone, capturing light in such a way that it became known as the Blue Hole. The Spanish were not the first to arrive there. Even today, the area yields remains of giant bison and mastodons and of Paleo-Indian hunters who passed through as long as ten thousand years ago.[4]

San Antonio's founders chose instead the firmer, more open and level land two miles west, around San Pedro Springs. Soon they saw the advantage of moving two miles south, between the narrow San Pedro Creek and the river on a site permitting access to water on both sides of town and more easily protected from Indian attacks. Here the river frequently doubled back on itself, allowing a density of homes and fields to be laid out in long, narrow lots both backing on a water source and fronting on a street.

San Antonio was planned in the manner officially prescribed for Spanish colonial towns, along a grid of streets converging on central plazas. Behind buildings lining the west side of Military Plaza, home of the Spanish garrison, ran San Pedro Creek. On the plaza's east side was the rear of the parish church of San Fernando, which fronted on a second square

Dozens of springs formed the lush headwaters of the San Antonio River two miles north of the center of town.

that came to be known as Main Plaza. A block to the northeast, the river's Great Bend curved sharply away toward the relocated Mission San Antonio de Valero—which became known as the Alamo—before returning, equally abruptly, a block to the southeast to flow southward.[5]

The Spanish were well accustomed to extending a meager water supply into flat, semiarid land like that beyond the river's gentle, narrow valley. For generations they had been fine-tuning the art of building acequias—irrigation ditches—using complex techniques brought to Spain by the Romans and enhancements imported from North Africa by the Moors. Of prime importance in the new settlement was digging these acequias, under the supervision of *acequiadores*, canal makers expert in engineering the gravity-driven waterways. By the mid-1770s seven acequia systems wove from the San Antonio River and San Pedro Creek down slight grades sometimes invisible to the untrained eye. New streets often followed the expanding network of twisting acequias, corrupting an orderly street

opposite page
The area beside San Pedro Springs, shown in the 1870s, was chosen as the first location of San Antonio when founders arrived in 1718.

left
Waters of the San Antonio River and San Pedro Creek were extended by an Old World system of acequias, which included such features as a 1740s stone aqueduct near Mission Espada, still in use, to carry irrigation water over a creek.

San Antonio's first permanent bridge over the river was the Old Red Bridge, below, built in 1842 at Commerce Street. The river's languid flow powered only small mills such as, right, an iron foundry, declared a public nuisance and forced to move because of its noise.

grid as the laws of gravity trumped the planning dictates of a distant Spanish king.[6]

Driven by river and creek, the acequias sustained San Antonio and its missions through a rapid succession of parent governments, from Spain to Mexico in the 1820s, to the Republic of Texas in the next decade, to the United States in the decade after that and then, with the Civil War, to the Confederacy and back to the United States.

By 1870, as San Antonio's population passed 12,000, the banks of its narrow river did not resemble at all the industrial banks in river cities of similar or larger size elsewhere in America. In the two miles from its headwaters to the southern edge of downtown, the river dropped only thirty-five feet, leaving its comparatively modest flow with insufficient force to power major mills and factories. River water did power small operations—a half dozen grist mills, two ice factories, a tannery, and two iron foundries, one of which created such a racket with its screeching water wheels and hammering that the city council declared the foundry a public nuisance and forced it to move.[7]

Ice manufactured from river water was a particular luxury. What little ice was available—often imported from Massachusetts—had to be hauled overland from ships docking at the coast, an expensive and cumbersome operation given the amount of insulation required. In the late 1860s, J. B. LaCoste opened the city's first successful ice plant on Losoya Street beside the river, and began providing ice—

resembling frozen snow—to the city's leading hotel, the Menger, for $50 a day.[8]

Such riverside outfits took up relatively small spaces, allowing the river banks to remain a random mix of stone and brick basement foundations of structures fronting on streets above. This random patchwork would significantly enhance the unique character of the future River Walk.

Larger river-driven industry did develop at the edges of downtown. To the north, two breweries—ultimately named Lone Star and Pearl—were housed in prominent buildings and used well water for making beer, sending runoff into the river. Near the southern edge of downtown, at the end of King William Street, the young German immigrant Carl Hilmar Guenther spotted an ideal location for a millrace where the river flowed southwest, then sharply doubled back to the northeast before again heading south. Just above this bend, Guenther had a millrace dug in 1859 from the higher parallel segment to the lower. He moved his eight-year-old flour-milling operation from Fredericksburg, and it eventually grew to fill the bend's inner loop.[9]

With little pollution from industry, the river maintained a healthy variety of marine life. In the mid-nineteenth century, John Blankenship, "the old lone fisherman of San Antonio," brought up from the Commerce Street bridge not only a regular supply of fish but, on one occasion, a six-foot eel. Crawfish were common, and small alligators made cameo appear-

left
Two 70-horsepower boilers were among the San Antonio Ice Company's equipment in its 1880s plant, left, beside the river.

below
Even when iron bridges were built, wagons continued to use Navarro Street's Old Mill Ford. The landmark Nat Lewis Mill and its millwheel, center, were on the site of the Hotel Contessa.

ances.[10] At the turn of the twentieth century, mussels thriving in hot mineral waters that fed the river near southern San Antonio's spas were found to contain freshwater pearls. This discovery led to a pearl rush "reminiscent of Klondike Days." Prospectors found up to three dozen pearls a day until the mussels were gone.[11]

Crossing the river could be a major problem as late as the 1880s. Before arrival of the railroad, iron and steel for bridges could be imported only with great difficulty, and street-level bridges were dispensed with whenever possible. The first permanent wagon bridge, the wooden "old red bridge," was built in 1842 across Commerce Street. Twenty years later there was

only one more street-level bridge, at Houston Street. Elsewhere in town, vehicles forded the river, and young boys quickly appeared to wash carriages in the river for a few cents. The water expanded the wood of the wheel frames, tightening them against the steel rims that passed for tires.[12]

Getting pedestrians across was a bit more complicated. Those unwilling or unable to wade or afraid to slip on stepping-stones could cross an assortment of flimsy, narrow plank bridges floating on airtight barrels with waist-level ropes or boards to grip. Banker John Twohig built a footbridge from his home on the northern bank of the Great Bend across to his office and his bank, which faced Commerce Street. Changes

Through the 1880s, most pedestrians crossed the river on wooden bridges floating on barrels. The one at right apparently crossed south of the Houston Street bridge. At far right, a dapper fisherman stands at the start of the Great Bend on the bridge of John Twohig, who crossed from his home through a door, locked and surrounded by barbed wire, to his office and bank on the opposite side, facing Commerce Street.

in the river level kept these floating footbridges from being inflexibly anchored at either end, and so were loosely chained to trees or posts. How far one had to step up or down to get on or off the bridge depended upon the water level at the time. During swiftly rising water, the chain on one side was released so the bridge could swing into the current, then be pulled back and rechained when the water receded.

Some children delighted in the crossing. "We would jump up and down on the footbridge," recalled one lady in later life, "and get ourselves thoroughly splashed with water."[13] Others were not as excited. "I always hated to cross this bridge," remembered another. "I crawled across it in rainy weather holding on tight on each side. At other times I always stayed right in the middle."[14]

On washday, women found it "much simpler" to bring clothes to the river rather than carrying water up the steep bank. Clothes were hung to dry on nearby brush.[15] A favorite laundrering spot was the widest part of the river, on the southern leg of the Great Bend above the Old Mill Ford near Nat Lewis's mill. Baptisms nearby could be counted upon to bring up "a chorus of hallelujahs" following the immersions.[16]

The rattletrap foundries, ramshackle backs of buildings, grist mills, fishermen, floating footbridges, drying clothes,

and hallelujahs were enough to qualify Frederick Law Olmsted's "odd and antiquated" assessment of San Antonio for the riverbanks alone. Even odder, though, were the floating bathhouses within the stream that eventually dotted the river for nearly a mile.[17] A special set of protocols developed around them and triggered a city council moral debate that split along ethnic lines.

Given San Antonio's lack of indoor plumbing and withering summer heat, the cool river was a great place to clean up. Bathing wear was often minimal or nonexistent. In the 1840s, visitors could report "quite a startling spectacle to see here, just above the bridge in the heart of the city, a number of Mexican women

Undergrowth was the place to hang out clothes washed at the widest place in the river, below Nat Lewis's millpond on the southern leg of the Great Bend.

Harper's New Monthly Magazine published the above engraving of bathhouses bobbing in the river in 1879. At right are muslin-covered bathhouses at the beginning of the Great Bend.

and girls bathing entirely naked, unconcerned about our presence."[18]

But such exposure did not suit mid-nineteenth century Victorian notions of modesty. The solution for those with homes backing on the river or nearby was to build enclosed bathhouses to shield bare skin from prying eyes.

Like the floating footbridges, bathhouses were set atop empty, airtight barrels. A framework, perhaps ten feet square, was sheathed in strips of muslin and covered by a roof, either flat and made of muslin or pitched and shingled, so that those on a high shore or in buildings above could not peer in. After entering through a muslin-covered door, bathers could hang their clothes on pegs and sit on benches. Wooden slat floors could be raised or lowered in the water, keeping adults or children at a safe depth. Men usually bathed early in the morning or late at night, with women and children following the afternoon siesta, though this was not always the case. "It was not unusual any time of day," according to one report, "to see a lady or gentleman making their way to the river with a towel, a bar of soap, and a change of clothes under their arm."[19]

What has been referred to as the earliest commercial bathhouse was a long affair, at first with no roof or floor, put in the river at the Old Mill Ford in 1852 by Sammy Hall, a lively entrepreneur who—with a fellow kilted Scotsman—drew crowds by playing bagpipes and dancing the Highland fling.[20] Another large public bathhouse rested on the natural rock floor around San Pedro Springs. Those for specific groups included one below the Ursuline Academy for students and resident sisters and another beside a German fraternal group's recreation area on Bowen's Island.[21]

As the prim folk moved to the cover of bath-houses, in the 1850s the city council outlawed nude public bathing in both the San Antonio River and San Pedro Creek, "despite the presence of two Mexican members."[22] Bathing, still permitted at fords during certain hours, was more common just outside city limits. There less inhibited men, women, and children, predominantly of Mexican heritage and "manifesting not the slightest regard for the curious glances of the passersby," could still bathe "without the annoy-ance of dresses."[23]

But the pressures of modernization swept in when the railroad finally reached San Antonio in 1877. A new underground water system required by the new growth opened in mid-1878, sending water from a new pump house below the headwa-ters springs through new

pipes up to a reservoir on a hill to the east. Gravity piped it downhill to town and into homes, which gained bathtubs. Bathhouses began disappearing, as did the downtown acequia system, another of San Antonio's oddities. Such changes fulfilled the prophecy of the visitor who wrote in 1859 that, until a railroad arrived, "San Antonio will be a peculiar and isolated city."[24]

It's hard to imagine the full scope of the trans-formation made possible by ready access to the rest of the world. Travel time between San Antonio and Houston and ports on the Texas coast dropped from days to hours. Freight no longer had to be strapped to awkward oxcarts negotiating rutted trails. The city's

Frank Leslie's Illustrated Newspaper ran this engraving entitled "Primitive bathing near San Antonio, from a sketch by our correspondent" in 1859.

appearance changed, as low buildings of such available materials as sun-baked adobe bricks or handcut limestone blocks were replaced by taller buildings built with inexpensively imported brick, steel, and even lumber, another former rare commodity in the region.

It also became easier to get around town. In 1871, six years before the railroad came, importing a single-span iron bridge to replace the wooden bridge over Houston Street was a major operation. The parts were cast in St. Louis, shipped by train to New Orleans and by boat to the Texas port of Indianola. "Some of the material was forty feet long and so heavy that it could only be transported on the largest wagons,"

recalled August Santleben, the legendary German-born freighting veteran who got the job. It took fourteen wagons to get the shipment to San Antonio. For his leg of the bridge's journey, Santleben was paid the considerable sum of $3,250.[25]

Navarro Street got two bridges a few years later from the King Iron Bridge Company of Cleveland, Ohio, both, like the Houston Street bridge, of simple utilitarian design. But an up-and-coming city deserved better, many San Antonians thought, now that materials could be brought in less expensively. A manufacturer with a flair for Victorian design turned up—the Berlin Bridge Company of East Berlin, Connecticut, then expanding its sales from the Northeast and mar-

keting its bridges throughout the West. Contracts were signed and rail shipments began.

Three distinctive Berlin bridges remain in use above the River Walk, on Augusta, Crockett, and South Presa streets.[26] A pedestrian bridge crossing Johnson Street near King William Street uses parts of a fourth—the celebrated Commerce Street Bridge. Its four ornamental iron corner spires once signaled to visitors on the main thoroughfare west from the Southern Pacific station that they were entering the main business district of an important city.[27]

As when other Berlin bridges were ceremoniously opened, in 1890 a fifteen-ton steamroller was driven onto a fifth Berlin bridge, a particularly elegant one for what is now called South St. Mary's Street. It was parked midway to prove the bridge's strength, as city and company officials posed beside it.

This bridge, however, touched off a political brawl. Centered between the arches at each end were plaques with the names of city officials—Mayor Bryan Callaghan's was the largest—lettered in gold paint. Mayor Callaghan may have been presiding over the most prosperous era yet in San Antonio, but some thought this bridge symbolized overspending by City Hall. In the next election Callaghan barely survived

charges of extravagance in what was remembered for years as the "Letters of Gold Campaign."[28]

As bathhouses disappeared, the still common rowboats gained some competition. In 1883, a pair of entrepreneurs planned to add to their two rowboats "a small-sized, low pressure steamboat" to carry twenty-five to fifty passengers from Houston Street around the Great Bend to the Mill Bridge. Six years later the small steamer *Hilda* was plying the route. In the 1890s, Finis F. Collins—a manufacturer of windmills, boilers, and such machinery at the prime northeast corner of Houston Street and the river—ran a daily steam launch, with Sunday trips every twenty minutes. "The water was crowded with other pleasure craft as well," according to one

Parking a steamroller on a Berlin Bridge Company iron bridge to demonstrate its strength was part of the dedication ceremony of the South St. Mary's Street bridge in 1890.

account, "but the steamer lorded it over the whole river."[29]

The era when tiny steamboats made San Antonio a sort of miniature New Orleans was short-lived. The level of the river and its ability to support boats, much less supply the city with water, was becoming increasingly uncertain as floods were becoming more serious.

The flooding problem came not from the San Antonio River itself but from the dry creeks that fed into it. In semiarid regions of Texas and the West,

This oil of the San Antonio River at the St. Mary's Street bridge was painted by Ida Weisselberg Hadra in 1883.

watersheds of such creeks with little vegetation to absorb and delay heavy rain allow a downpour to send a wall of water raging many miles downstream into areas with no rainfall, inundating, without warning, whatever happens to be in its path. The San Antonio River was particularly vulnerable to sudden runoff from Olmos Creek, which drains an area of some thirty-four square miles to the northwest into the river just below the headwaters, and, to the west, from Alazan, Apache, and Martinez creeks, their combined twenty-three square mile drainage area crossing western San Antonio and joining San Pedro Creek and then the river just south of town.

San Antonio's earliest recorded equivalent of a hundred-year-flood came in July 1819, when what was reported as a *culebra de agua*—a serpent or snake of water, a "cloudburst"—fell into the drainage area of Olmos Creek. Its waters surged into the San Antonio River, already swollen by rain. Floodwaters from the river and San Pedro Creek rampaged through Main and Military plazas, washing away a dozen adobe and stone buildings. Water was reported five feet high within San Fernando Church. Afterward, the parish priest presided over funerals for sixteen flood victims, ten of them Indian children. Antonio María Martínez, the last governor of Texas under Spain, moved the Spanish soldiers from the wreckage of their barracks on Military Plaza to La Villita, soon recognized for its higher elevation as one of the finer places in town to live.[30]

Scarcely a quarter century later, in 1845, San Antonio was struck by a less disastrous but still severe flood. Mayor Edward Dwyer then made an ambitious proposal: build a dam near the end of Olmos Creek to hold back the worst of the floodwaters. Dwyer's successor brought up the idea again seven years later, when flooding sent the river eight feet above its normal level and into the streets.[31]

But it took one more flood before city government went so far as to form a study committee. That happened after a flood on March 26, 1865, in which at least three people drowned. One spectator, Albert Maverick, then eleven, remembered wading "everywhere" after the flood and seeing the wooden Houston Street Bridge "like an island" in the receding floodwaters. Caught behind its midstream supports was "a great mass of driftwood forming a dam and backing up the water."[32] Although rainfall preceding the flood of 1865 was the same as in the flood of 1845, floodwaters had risen six feet higher, and loss of life and property damage were much worse.

A dam on Olmos Creek was proposed once again, along with a counterproposal to divert floodwaters by digging a channel west and south to Alazan Creek to bypass the center of town.[33] The committee of engineers placed blame for the increased flooding squarely on new development. In the twenty-year interim between the two floods, Texas had joined the United States, and San Antonio's population had mushroomed. Shrunken by political and military upheav-

left
The lone surviving riverside industry is C. H. Guenther's Pioneer Flour Mills, shown in 1909 beside his home, enlarged and now a restaurant at the far southern end of the River Walk.

right
St. Mary's Catholic Church, built in 1859, was a riverside landmark until it was replaced after the flood of 1921.

FOURTH STEET BRIDGE,
SAN ANTONIO RIVER.

The crossing where Fourth Street joins Lexington Avenue became the northern terminus of Robert Hugman's future River Walk.

als, the number of residents had dropped from 2,000 in Spanish times to 800 by the time Texas joined the United States in 1845. Within twenty more years, however, the population was 8,000. Floodwaters in 1865 were especially made worse, the committee found, by new walls narrowing the channels of the river and San Pedro Creek, by midstream supports of new bridges, and by midtown's Concepción Acequia diversion dam, which both raised and then slowed floodwaters. Behind them, such dams held deposits of mud that permanently raised the river level.[34]

The engineers' advice was heeded, at least in part. The wagon bridge over Commerce Street was replaced with a new span that lacked its predecessor's midstream supports. Four years and two lesser floods later, in 1869, the Concepción Acequia diversion dam was removed.[35]

In the two decades following the 1865 flood, San Antonio's population tripled, with the aid of the new railroad, to 25,000 residents. Development not only increased runoff during floods; it added to the problem of too little water during droughts. The water system that replaced the acequias was expanded, but its supply still came only from springs at the river's headwaters. By August 1887 the river suffered from "am almost unprecedented lack of water" as drought depleted the springs. It touched off widespread alarm. Waterworks officials pleaded with city council to limit commercial and industrial water use and watering of lawns and gardens.[36]

Many San Antonians blamed the cause, incorrectly, as it turned out, not on lack of rainfall but on undergrowth and debris, which residents believed prevented water from flowing up through the springs and down through the river. The council came up with $3,000 to clear away logs and growth. The approach was supported by the San Antonio *Light*, which editorialized against such "artificial obstructions" as dams and debris dumped into the river and "natural obstructions"—brush, trees, and accumulations of silt.[37]

In the meantime, artesian wells had been discovered as a seemingly unlimited source of new water in California and elsewhere in the West. By the mid-1880s the Fort Worth area had some 200 artesian wells. They required no pumping; the water "just flowed over the top." In 1887–88, the first two artesian wells in San Antonio were drilled into the Austin limestone aquifer near the West End subdivision, and helped supply the new body of water now known as Woodlawn Lake. Nearly a dozen more such wells were soon drilled in surrounding Bexar County.[38]

As the drought worsened and the headwaters continued to drop, San Antonio icemakers found the water quality declining and compromising the quality of their ice. In 1888–89, the first documented well flowing from the Edwards Aquifer was drilled by the Crystal Ice Company, near the San Antonio River at Avenue B and Eighth Street. The drilling took five months. The company followed its success with three more wells.[39]

George Brackenridge, who headed the San Antonio Water Works, gave little heed to those who thought the problem was clogged springs and believed the

problem was simply lack of available water. He tried drilling an artesian well as a backup supply near his water company's hilltop reservoir. Perhaps because of the high elevation, it was unsuccessful. Hoping to strike water at a lower elevation, the water works purchased land downtown at the southwest corner of Market Street and the river. There, in 1891, at a depth of 890 feet, drillers struck water with such pressure that it spouted fifteen to twenty feet into the air and blew out rocks, according to witnesses, "as large as a man's head." The well began producing three million gallons of water a day.[40]

Within seven years there were some seventy artesian wells throughout Bexar County, all of

A crew of boys kept wagons washed in the Old Mill Ford beneath the southern Navarro Street bridge. The water expanded the wooden wheels and tightened them to the metal rims.

them being blamed, accurately, for lowering available surface water and worsening the effects of yet another drought, which began in the spring of 1897. The headwaters springs, which flowed at 24,000 cubic feet per minute when the water works opened, dropped to as low as 2,000 cubic feet per minute and began drying up. Downstream, the river dwindled

Natural pressure forced water over the top of new artesian wells, soon drilled in such numbers that the water table declined and springs feeding the San Antonio River began to dry up.

to a trickle through the slime of refuse no longer carried away by a swift current.

Brackenridge sought regulation of artesian drilling to limit such declines, but was unsuccessful. His personal reaction was that he could no longer live nearby. In 1897 he sold his estate to the Sisters of Charity of the Incarnate Word for their motherhouse and academy. The land, some of it now within the southern limits of the city of Alamo Heights, later became the campus of the University of the Incarnate Word.[41]

Wrote Brackenridge to a friend: "I have seen this bold, bubbling, laughing river dwindle and fade away. This river is my child and it is dying, and I cannot stay here to see its last gasps. . . . I must go."[42] Brackenridge built a larger home a few years later on a new estate a mile and a half east.

Despite all the hand-wringing over the declining river, there were those who could look beyond the slime and the silt to another day. Why, wondered an anonymous writer to the San Antonio *Express* in the dry August of 1887, shouldn't the riverbanks become a park?

The banks "could be converted into flower beds, and pleasure boats [could] afford recreation to hundreds," the writer believed, with remarkable prescience. "Many of our citizens are prone to look entirely upon the utility side of every question, and the river as an ornament would be likely to excite ridicule, but . . . our river would be the crown jewel of Texas."[43]

You will find auntie on the steps

San Antonio River - College Grove.
College and Academy of the Incarnate Word.   Alamo Heights.   San Antonio.   Texas.

Despite a declining water table that dried up most springs at the river's headwaters, a dam restored this pond on what became the campus of the University of the Incarnate Word. "You will find auntie on the steps," wrote an Irish-born nun on the front of this postcard to her family back home.

2
BUILDING THE RIVER PARK

San Antonio in 1900 was about to enter a dynamic decade and a half. Once again San Antonio was the largest city in the largest state. Its population leapt beyond 50,000, passing Galveston's, as new residents poured in with an influx of fresh ideas and the energy and talent to carry them out.

As the new century's second decade unfolded, a broad reform movement uncorked by the sudden death of a longtime machine mayor was, in turn, slowed by the sudden death of his progressive successor. The San Antonio River was going dry with increasing frequency. Engineering plans to bury the river were, however, scrapped after a groundswell of complaints combined with floods that kept reviving the river and sending water over its banks and into the streets.

No longer did San Antonio evolve in eccentric isolation. If residents were not on the cutting edge of trends, they were at least implementing many of them, albeit a bit behind the rest of the nation. One significant advance was a river park, briefly a focal point for civic events that foreshadowed those along the future River Walk. It was achieved as a key element of local reforms during San Antonio's belated entry into the City Beautiful movement, a municipal planning theme at its peak nationally from 1900 to 1910.

Reformers had a solid base upon which to plan such a park. River beautification calls first made after the drought of 1887 were rising in a crescendo. Some storms briefly restored a healthy flow to the river, but the headwaters springs had not run for most of the drought years of 1897–99, nor did they in the summer of 1900.[1] Only runoff originating from wells of two breweries kept any water in the river downtown. Increased drilling of artesian wells to put more water in the municipal reservoir simply made things worse along the river by lowering the water table and reducing the springs even further. With little flow to carry off garbage and refuse accumulating on the muddy bottom, city sanitary inspectors ordered those piping wastewater into the river to stop. More calls came to clean things up.[2]

A break came when a wet season began in November 1902 and culminated in a flood on February 26, 1903. Floodwaters briefly got within twenty-five inches of the record set in 1865, though

opposite page
Horse-drawn and motor-driven vehicles mingle on Crockett Street above San Antonio's new river park, completed in 1914, as seen from the Navarro Street bridge west to St. Mary's Street.

they caused less damage. They reached a depth of two and a half feet on St. Mary's Street, flooding basements of adjacent businesses and homes before moving downstream. A number of small homes were swept away. The only warning came at 2 a.m. that day, when an engineer on duty at a waterworks pump house two miles upstream phoned Fire Chief William G. Tobin to say that floodwaters were heading toward town. Tobin quickly mobilized his force to prepare for rescues. There were no drownings.[3]

The next year the river was drying up once again. Those San Antonians clinging to the belief that it was all because of clogged springs and a debris-choked riverbed recalled stories passed down from Spanish

High waters on January 10, 1900, did not deter a few wagons from using the Old Mill Ford. The view is west from Navarro Street toward the Bexar County Courthouse. City Hall's clock tower is visible on the center horizon.

times, when severe droughts threatened the river's flow into acequias. At such times, it was said, families assembled at assigned places. "With all manner of agricultural and farm implements known in that day," they scraped away accumulations of mud down to the gravel riverbed, and springs once more bubbled from the bottom. Figuring that was worth a try, firemen took their hoses and gave the riverbed a scouring. The river gradually rose, whether from the cleaning or from new rains. Weekend boaters again plied the river, its banks overhung with "boughs, cresses and ferns."[4]

But dense branches and foliage obscured the diminished river. The street department was sent in to remove some trees to open things up. In the course of its work in the summer of 1904, one crew cut down two large willows which others quickly declared had been "magnificent."

For the first time, the depth of support for a beautified river was revealed. To protest the overly ambitious trimming, the newly formed Civic Improvement Association delivered to city council chambers "a full hundred citizens of the staid, sober and substantial kind that does not venture out except upon occasions of real merit."

A series of indignant speakers took the street commissioner to task for not having obeyed council instructions issued following an earlier such incident. Mayor Pro Tem Vories Brown satisfied the crowd by reassigning the job to Park Commissioner Ludwig Mahncke and by announcing that new grass and trees would be planted beside the river. Association leaders thanked Brown and also the press, "for its efforts in behalf of preserving the river which has made San Antonio noted abroad."[5]

City officials, "uniformly favorable to the river," promised "to beautify the stream and protect it in every manner possible." Mahncke contracted with a nursery in adjacent Kendall County for several hundred cypress saplings from the banks of the Guadalupe River to be transplanted to the banks of the San Antonio River, where many grew into some of the towering shade trees lining the River Walk. Penalties were set for unauthorized cutting of riverside trees and shrubs, and authorities prepared to defend the city's river property line against encroachments.[6]

Energized by their bout with city hall, San Antonians began making the river part of their civic festivities, including the annual spring festival, which evolved into the extravaganza of parades and events taking up the entire third week of each April. The festival traditionally began with a masked king's arrival at a railroad station to greet the public. This time, on the evening of April 24, 1905, the king arrived on the river. Waters from heavy rains subsided in time to permit a safe voyage for a flower-bedecked, torchlit flotilla, its

In 1903 the lower level of the Clifford Building at the Commerce Street bridge was inundated in the worst flooding since 1865. During the next year, over-zealous trimming of overgrowth along the river, below, set off a wave of protest.

royal barge decorated in silver and gold. It was San Antonio's first river parade.

In a scene "not unlike the ancient glories of the Bosphorous in the day of the Caesars," a steady blast of trumpets heralded the fleet's arrival at the landing along Tobin Terrace, the newly-landscaped banks below Crockett Street between St. Mary's and Navarro streets apparently named for Fire Chief William Tobin, whose crews had cleaned the river. Crowds cheered as the king was greeted by the commodore of the whimsically named Alamo Yacht Club and ascended with his entourage to the street for an illuminated parade.[7]

Tobin Terrace was the name given to the section of the river beautified by a cleaning in 1904 under the direction of Fire Chief William Tobin. The bank at left has since been cleared away for arched entrances beneath Crockett Street to the Watermark Hotel and Aztec on the River.

The next month, the Tobin Terrace landing was the setting for a Memorial Day service organized by the Women's Relief Corps in honor of deceased sailors. "At the proper time during the exercises, a number of children led by a little boy holding an American flag aloft stepped on a floating barge," a newspaper reported. "As the barge glided gently along with the rippling current, the children showered flowers upon the water, and those along the bank did likewise."[8]

Although the spring festival skipped the river the next year, in 1907 plans were made for a gala riverside Carnival of Venice. But uncertain conditions of the river, barely overcome two years before, made that river parade the last for nearly thirty years. A temporary dam built to raise the water level was washed out by a cloudburst the day of the parade. Events were postponed for three days while the Alamo Yacht Club's boats, damaged in the washout, were repaired and the dam was rebuilt.

Finally, on April 19, 1907, thousands gathered on bridges and banks to watch the king parade down the river. Strings of colored lights crisscrossed the river and glowed in its trees from Houston Street to the Mill Bridge. Each of the dozen skiffs, lit with strings of Japanese lanterns, carried costumed "Indians and their squaws," who appeared "very grotesque" in the light of the torches. A searchlight in the lead boat played on the crowds and on the river. As the barge of the masked king—later revealed to be real estate mogul John H. Kirkpatrick—drew up to the Tobin

Terrace landing, the other boats passed in review, then turned back toward Houston Street. A band played "See the Conquering Hero Comes," fireworks on the riverbank went off, "and the crowd shouted itself hoarse."[9]

Events directly involving the river may have begun a long hiatus, but the river was not ignored during fiestas. In April 1910, "many thousands of tri-colored electric globes" were strung over the river and along its banks in the business district. As its float in the street parade, the Civic Improvement League built a twenty-foot canoe, its "rowers" representing the old and the new. On the canoe was a banner emblazoned with the words, "What the Civic Improvement League is going to do with the San Antonio River."[10]

True to a headline declaring "Public Wants River To Receive First Attention," the league began to spruce up three sections with new grass, flowers, and shrubs. Permanent lighting across the river was planned. An island below the Mill Bridge was to become a garden of roses and ferns and the riverbed was to be smoothed to a uniform depth to make its flow more regular. Public baths would make up for the loss of deep swimming holes.[11]

During the dry summer of 1910, however, the river slowed to a trickle once more.[12] A writer to the *Express* complained that he had gone for a mile downriver and counted eight privies emptying into the river, which he estimated "is about one foot deep in water and another foot deep in filth and muck and

slime." If the Publicity League was spending $50,000 to bring people to San Antonio "for health and recreation and pleasure," he suggested that the group "spend a little more money and give the people what they came here for."[13]

By now it was becoming obvious that make-shift efforts to deal with the river would not be sufficient. Indeed, the river was seen as part of a larger municipal picture by those who were grasping the elements of an agenda developed nationally in the City Beautiful movement. Though they had no formal organization, City Beautiful advocates in various major cities had developed an agenda that combined civic and environmental activism with political reform to improve the surroundings and, therefore, the lot of all citizens, yielding economic

The blurred reproduction of an early newspaper photograph gives an impressionistic view of this Memorial Day ceremony at Tobin Terrace in 1905, when children on a barge scattered flowers on the river in memory of deceased sailors from San Antonio.

rewards. They developed, in the process, many principles of modern city planning.

A properly appointed modern city needed a stately civic center, parks, and boulevard systems, thought the movement's supporters. Streets needed to be paved, billboards restrained, trees planted, and playgrounds established. Supporters realized that the municipal bond issues these required could usually be achieved only through political reform, so political action became a necessary part of the reformer's agenda.[14]

By the middle of the decade, progressive San Antonians believed that their city should act in a manner befitting its new importance and take its rank among other cities embracing City Beautiful reforms, including Kansas City, Denver, Seattle, even Dallas. Like other cities, San Antonio suffered from unpaved streets, an inadequate sewer system, and undirected growth, to say nothing of the perplexing case of the river. Soon a large number of San Antonians, led mostly by recent arrivals, launched what was perhaps the most broadly targeted reform movement in San Antonio's history.

True to the City Beautiful template, an initial target was city hall. San Antonio politics had been dominated for some twenty-five years by Bryan Callaghan, the mayor off and on for half that time. The response to his name in gold on the St. Mary's Street bridge reinforced Callaghan's sense of the importance of municipal penury to political survival. Callaghan kept taxes low and held few bond elections. If San Antonians wanted more paved streets, new gas and sewer lines, or other amenities, they could come up with ways to pay for them privately. City hall might be falling behind in basic services, but it was not going to move forward any faster.[15]

Against that backdrop, in 1909 a political reform committee was organized, then a Commission Government League, to set the basis for a more forward-looking city government. The top goal was a change in the city charter to replace ward-based aldermen with at-large commissioners, who would each be assigned specific urban services. In the heated campaign that followed, reformers pledged to "knock into smithereens the cloud of Callaghanism which has hovered over San Antonio for the past quarter of a century."[16] A record 80 percent of San Antonio voters turned out for the charter election in February 1911. Of 14,000 votes cast, the proposed charter was defeated by a margin of only 160.[17]

The narrow defeat sent reformers into even higher gear. A host of adhoc improvement groups arose and began work. A Playground and Recreation Association raised funds to purchase and equip a Buena Vista Street plot as a playground. A Civic Improvement Art League was formed. A Coliseum League began raising funds for a 12,000-seat coliseum. The Woman's Club and the Chamber of Commerce proposed a coordinating Civic Improvement Federation "to promote the health and beauty of the city." The Alamo Film Company

planned a movie to show even "in other countries, . . . giving the widest publicity to the general plan for keeping San Antonio sanitary and attractive." The City Federation of Women's Clubs gained a measure of success against "the billboard nuisance" by persuading city council to pass an ordinance curtailing the growing epidemic of billboards.[18]

In the midst of all the activity, battle lines were drawn over the very existence downtown of the San Antonio River. On one side were advocates of a dramatically beautified river—even including a river walk—led by progressive citizens and the two daily newspapers. On the other were businessmen armed with an engineering report declaring that the river could be buried in a tunnel beneath downtown. The former river channel would be converted to prime real estate.

River advocates ratcheted up their campaign early in 1911, as the *Light* contrasted a photo of still overgrown riverbanks south of the major Houston Street thoroughfare with a rendering of the same scene proposed by the prominent London-born San Antonio architect Alfred Giles. The drawing showed boats being rowed on a channeled river as pedestrians passed by on sidewalks on either side. The *Light* wrote: "A comparison of the two pictures . . . shows in a striking manner how easily one of the ugliest spots in the city can be converted into one of the most attractive."[19]

The competing *Express* agreed. "Few cities possess so great a natural asset as a winding, tree-shaded stream such as the San Antonio River," the paper editorialized. "Its sinuous course through the city . . . elicits the admiration of visitors, even though the stream has dwindled to a sluggish current running through neglected banks over a riverbed covered with slime and silt." But with "its banks beautified,

The beautified riverbanks at the St. Mary's Street bridge below the Oblate Fathers' home, next door to St. Mary's Catholic Church, were chosen by the Missouri Kansas & Texas Railway for this cover of a travel promotion publication in 1911.

dredged and made a clear, swift stream as it was in 'the old days,' it would be the chief factor in the San Antonio Beautiful."[20]

The river, however, did not cooperate. That summer it went dry not only at the headwaters but all the way down to the city. Deep cracks opened in its dried mud. Runoff from wells used by the two breweries at the northern edge of the city kept some water flowing through downtown, but the most visible stretch of the river, between Houston and Commerce streets, was branded one of the worst looking areas of the city. "Day by day," reported the *Light*, "it offends the eyes of thousands of people as they cross the Houston Street bridge."[21]

Opponents of the river sensed it was time to strike.

As enthusiasm for a beautified river grew, and as a plan to fill in the river channel was itself buried, noted architect Alfred Giles in 1911 came up with this drawing of how a river walk might look.

Shortening the path of the declining river through downtown had been discussed for years. After the flood in 1903, architect Francis Bowen suggested a new channel cut straight through the heart of the city, eliminating the Great Bend. This would not only improve runoff, "it would do away with a circuitous dirty river as well . . . and give a great deal of space to some better purpose." As time passed, the idea grew in some quarters that the river, by then "little more than a creek," should be "closed up and transformed into a driveway."[22]

Now, in the late summer of 1911, a group of downtown businessmen hungry for new space for development revealed a conclusion by the young engineer Willard Simpson, commissioned to do a study of the matter.[23] Simpson concluded that most of the river downtown could be filled in, and that the river and its floodwaters could be carried through an underground conduit from Travis Street north of downtown past Nueva Street to the south. The ugly stretch between Houston and Commerce streets would disappear, as would the entire Great Bend. Nine high-maintenance bridges, six of them crossing the bend, could be eliminated. A strip of land some seventy feet wide and more than a mile long could be sold for commercial development.[24]

Beautification advocates countered quickly. The stature of businessmen in their ranks indicated that the business community was hardly unanimous in wanting the river buried. On the evening of September

26, 1911, three dozen citizens gathered at Chamber of Commerce headquarters to form the San Antonio River Improvement Association. Banker Thomas L. Conroy declared there had to be a way to revive the river, "and it must be found." The president of the City Federation of Women's Clubs, Emma (Mrs. M. J.) Bliem, promised the help of her constituency in beautifying the river. The new River Improvement Association president, hotelier M. B. Hutchins, assured city council that his group had "no intent to inject politics into the movement;" members simply wanted to show that people were "deeply interested" in seeing water back in the river and in having the river cleaned and beautified.[25]

Such an assurance was sufficient for the tight-fisted Mayor Callaghan to approve installation of a fifty-horsepower pump at an abandoned artesian well by the river at the northern end of Brackenridge Park, albeit at no cost to the city. The mayor refused to allow the city to pay for a shelter over the pump and vetoed a $500 prize for plans for a series of dams, floodgates, and flushing devices. He did authorize city laborers to clear fallen trees and undergrowth from the dry upper riverbed.[26]

The new pumps were soon pumping 500 gallons a minute into the riverbed, then 1,000 gallons, then 1,500. The pump ran for two and a half hours at a stretch, then ten, then twenty. Curious San Antonians flocked to the site as water slowly filled the riverbed's deep holes and cracks. Long-dormant springs began

Water pouring from increasing numbers of artesian wells met the needs of a growing city, but lowered the water table and caused the San Antonio River to go dry during droughts.

to reappear. But the millions of gallons were not reaching the river's downtown banks, nor even, a half mile north of Josephine Street, "Page's fishing hole," which nevertheless on its own suddenly brimmed once more with "beautiful blue water."[27]

Miles downstream, farmers who had given up their crops for lost saw water inexplicably fill the two old mission acequias. A reporter dispatched to the scene found that it "brought out the greenness and changed the appearance of everything in this valley." Workers were too busy harvesting to speculate on whether the unexpected water surfaced from some unknown underground channel starting near Brackenridge Park.[28]

But other than getting a little water into the river, reformers had little luck with their broad agenda against a recalcitrant city hall. City council defeated a street-paving ordinance by a vote of seven to five. A plan to dredge the river and remove accumulated

Architect Harvey Page
suggested paving the
river bottom with
interlocking concrete
slabs and crossing
it with monumental
bridges.

refuse met with familiar equivocations, as did pro-posals for the city to pay for continued pumping and to dam the river and to make a park along its banks within city limits.[29]

Suddenly, in mid-1912, halfway through his seventh term in office, Mayor Bryan Callaghan died. Six weeks later, reform candidate Augustus H. Jones, a rancher and financial backer of the new St. Anthony Hotel, was elected mayor. The old political machine was out. The Citizen's League was in.

Mayor Jones wasted little time. Less than two weeks after his inauguration, he took what one news-paper termed "the first big step to make this a City Beautiful and a Greater San Antonio"—appointment of a City Plan Committee. Boston, Chicago, Denver,

Cleveland, and several dozen other cities already had formal plans. Why shouldn't San Antonio? "San Antonio can be made the most beautiful place in the country," Jones said, "and when that is done there will be a rush of homeseekers from all parts of the country."[30]

To chair the City Plan Committee the mayor picked rising young architect Atlee B. Ayres. Reformer Thomas Conroy was made vice chairman. Members agreed with Civic Improvement League director T. Noah Smith, who insisted, "No complete plan could be adopted that would not include the preserving and beautifying of the river. The river cannot be beautiful through the business district if buildings line its course to the water's edge. . . . No city plan will be complete that does not include space along its banks for flowers, colonnades, pergolas, etc. in addition to the parks and plazas we now have [elsewhere]."[31]

The depth of the problem was outlined by River Commissioner George Surkey, who charged that the river, despite city ordinances, "has become a dumping ground." He asked the City Plan Committee, "How can the river be kept clean when each day every-thing from an old whip to a horse blanket is thrown into it?"[32]

Ayres made river beautification his top priority along with upgrading facilities and rescuing dying trees in Brackenridge and San Pedro parks. The day after his appointment he declared the river's width should be made uniform with walls, its banks terraced and planted with flowers and trees. There were to be footpaths, lighted at night, along the river. Concrete bridges "built along classic lines" should replace high-maintenance bridges. The project would be like those "carried out with a wonderfully gratifying effect throughout Europe."[33]

Four days later, the City Plan Committee unanimously endorsed a plan unveiled by one of its members, another leading San Antonio architect, Washington, D.C.–born Harvey L. Page.

Page, it turned out, had been pondering the subject for some time. Basic to his plan were interlocking, "indestructible" reinforced concrete slabs four inches thick, four feet in width, and eight feet in height, sloping toward the channel's center to create a faster midstream current to speed floodwaters through the city. The concrete slabs would line the river for thirteen miles. Page estimated they could be built on site and hoisted into place for no more than the cost of a sidewalk of similar size. Dams to preserve the water level would include small locks for dredge boats to maintain "an absolutely sanitary stream" and would "do away with all chances of breeding disease."

Also, streets crossing the river would get decorative concrete bridges. Numerous benches would turn the banks into "a vast park," while "at night myriads of electric bulbs will shine from the trees while Mexicans dressed in the garb of Aztec Indians will paddle canoes, filled with tourists. . . . [and] stopping at picturesque mission landings for refreshments. . . . Firefly lights playing in the trees and in the shrubbery along the banks, with here and there a moonlight effect from a larger lamp, . . . [will] make the San Antonio River a bit of fairyland and unlike anything in the world." Page estimated his plan would cost no more than $1 million and would be

Developer Alvah Davis commissioned James Converse to do this design for a river walk.

Rather than go to the expense of numerous private plans for river design, the city had its own river commissioner, George Surkey, begin simple channel walls and riverside plantings in 1913. When Surkey ran out of stone for the walls, he recycled some being torn from facades of buildings then being cut back for the widening of Commerce Street, below.

repaid by canoe concession fees. As an added benefit, the value of private riverside property would rise.[34]

The *Express* endorsed Page's proposals with enthusiasm: "The San Antonio River may again be the pride of all San Antonio, and this stream may be made the most unique in the United States. . . . The famous canal of Venice will not compare with the San Antonio River, and tourists will come thousands of miles to see this city and this stream."[35] One headline writer was sufficiently impressed to predict, "City Beautiful In Sight."

Other imaginative concepts continued to come up, notably one illustrated for real estate man Alvah B. Davis by James N. Converse. Davis suggested lighted sidewalks twelve feet wide on both sides of the river between Houston and St. Mary's streets, arguing that such a promenade would make river-level frontage at least as valuable as frontage on the streets above.[36]

In the wake of this enthusiasm, little more was heard of the Simpson plan to bury the river for another nine years.

In the first months of the Jones administration, it seemed hard not to get carried away over the reforms that seemed to lie just ahead. Noah Smith took charge of a committee to reform the structure of city government. The council, instead of quibbling over costs, summarily appropriated $1,000 to restore a pump beside the river in Brackenridge Park. Architect Harvey Page and two others went to work on beautifying the river below the Mill Bridge. For a master plan, the City Plan Committee recommended hiring George E. Kessler, one of the nation's leading planners and City Beautiful advocates, who was then at work on plans for Kansas City and Dallas. A $6,000 public fund was set up to pay his fee. Mayor Jones contributed the first $50.[37]

True to his promise, soon after taking office Augustus Jones authorized the first major beautifica-

tion project on the San Antonio River. As river commissioner he appointed George Surkey, a Missouri-born, one-time railroad fireman, engineer, and roundhouse foreman who had been a city councilman before going into real estate. With city funds, Surkey began a version of Page's plan, scaled down in scope and cost despite excitement over the scheme. Low concrete-covered rock walls—dubbed the "Surkey Sea Walls"—established a uniform width for the downtown channel. Next would come sodding and planting. Surkey sought a new artesian well to double the river's flow.[38]

The city considered straightening the river at opposite ends of downtown. Where the southern leg of the Great Bend doubled back to define Bowen's Island, a developer got permission to dig a cutoff channel to eliminate part of the switchback. The old section would remain filled with water as "a large natatorium and wading pool" for the Sans Souci Amusement Park, to be "one of the south's most elaborate and best-equipped." The erstwhile riverbank would become a beach.[39]

No agreement, however, was reached on a proposal by developer Paul Knittel to shorten a circuitous bend just north of downtown and gain title to the former riverbed for the proposed coliseum. Knittel also dared to suggest eliminating the Great Bend, not with a buried conduit but with a canal following the course originally planned for the north-south conduit. Said he: "Just think of the improvement that would follow

the filling up of the riverbed all round that long sweep that channel now follows."[40]

Less than eight months after it began, the Jones administration ended with the sudden death of the 53-year-old mayor. But Camelot-on-the-River did not come to a halt. Mayor Pro Tem Albert Steves left office nearly two months later having advocated continuing beautification of the river and building a dam on Olmos Creek both for flood control and as a reservoir.[41]

Despite the absence of Augustus Jones, the Citizen's League made a clean sweep in the next election, winning every council seat in a victory seen as a mandate for a long-awaited bond issue. The mayor-elect, former district attorney Clinton L. Brown, inspected municipal improvements in Kansas City, Dallas, and Fort Worth. A $3.5 million bond

The city's river beautification project was interrupted in 1913 by two major floods. The first, in October, drew this unbelieving crowd to the Houston Street bridge.

issue soon passed, providing funds for new bridges over the river.

As River Commissioner George Surkey continued work on his "sea walls," his budget request was cut by nearly half. He ran out of stone in mid-1913 and was reduced to recycling rocks from building fronts razed to widen Commerce Street. Commerce Street's landmark iron bridge with its four spires was moved downstream to Johnson Street to make way for a wider concrete bridge.[42]

During the last three months of 1913, San Antonians were distracted from work on Commerce Street and the river, and from just about everything else, when not one but two floods sent water up into downtown streets for the first time in ten years.

Streetcars were navigating the corner of Houston and St. Mary's streets past the Hertzberg clock as October 1913 floodwaters receded from their downtown crest of three feet, while residents beside Alazan Creek, below, in near western San Antonio, were beginning to deal with the loss of homes and other damage.

Heavy rains were creating problems by the last day of September. Cities in central and east Texas were isolated by floodwaters and railroad bridges were washed out, disrupting train service into San Antonio. On October 1, a record twenty-four-hour rainfall of 7.08 inches began that sent waters of the San Antonio River and San Pedro and Alazan creeks rising two to four feet an hour.[43]

At 2:30 p.m. the river overflowed into "a surging mass of muddy waters" down St. Mary's Street into the center of downtown, filling adjacent cellars along the way. Water poured into the basement of the Gunter Hotel from sidewalk grates and air shafts "with a roar like that of Niagara Falls." Within half an hour the hotel's boiler room was out of service, electric lights were out, and the hotel's barber shop, wine room, and baggage rooms were inundated. Water rose to within inches of the floor of the lobby overhead. There were similar scenes at neighboring businesses and homes.[44]

A call from Mayor Brown to the commander at Fort Sam Houston met with an immediate response. Within thirty minutes, a cavalry troop and a field artillery unit with wagons and ambulances were on the scene. Fire Chief Phil Wright abandoned his auto and a buggy and then wore out three horses as he directed the rescue effort and made rescues himself. Marooned families got on the phone to city hall, giving the mayor and city officials based there "a mighty big job."[45]

Floodwaters held their crest of three feet at Houston and St. Mary's streets for two hours, then began to subside. Crowds watched from bridges and

individuals waded and romped in water-filled streets. Steam fire engines began pumping out basements. Total damage was estimated at $250,000. Despite frequent reports of drownings there were only four casualties in Bexar County, a mother and her three young children swept away while fleeing their home far downstream near San José mission.[46]

Hardly two months later, on December 4, heavy rain fell across south and central Texas, particularly over Waco. Though less heavy than in October, damage was more severe, for it fell on ground saturated by two weeks of rain. Flooding caused 177 deaths and damage exceeding $8.5 million.[47]

In San Antonio, rain fell gently throughout the evening of December 3, then at one o'clock the next morning turned into an hour-long downpour. It

A lone pedestrian venturing across the street just missed a bicyclist swishing through the October 1913 floodwaters at Houston and St. Mary's streets, above. Below, a horse-drawn moving van waited for traffic to clear at St. Mary's and Travis streets.

When another flood struck San Antonio in December 1913, Fort Sam Houston again dispatched cavalry troops, a few shown at top left at the corner of Houston and St. Mary's streets. The photographer could turn to his right for the scene at top right, from the middle of Houston Street down St. Mary's Street toward the bridge. At lower left, two men on a balcony of the Southwestern Bell Telephone Company building on Travis Street got a view of the scene west to St. Mary's Street, an intersection where activity is more closely pictured at lower right.

Houston Street traffic in the foreground resumed, upper left, as December 1913 floodwaters receding down Navarro Street flowed off the Navarro Street bridge, lower left, and into the flood-swollen river. Water in Houston Street's Princess Theater, upper right, forced cancellation of the silent film features *Trapped in the Castle of Mystery* and *Love vs. Law*. Next door, the Gunter Hotel's guests had been evacuated in horse-drawn buses, leaving the lobby to a lone clerk, blurred by a cameraman's slow film.

slowed, then intensified again. High waters coursing down Olmos Creek caught the attention of residents of Alamo Heights, who telephoned warnings downstream to the fire and police chiefs. To rescue citizens and guard property, soldiers were once again called from Fort Sam Houston, and two local companies of the Texas National Guard were mobilized.[48]

As in October, the San Antonio River jumped its banks onto North St. Mary's Street, creating a lake south of Martin Street as it ignored the left turn into the bend to follow a straighter path—through downtown and back into the river below Market Street. Water again flowed into basements, but many of these had been left empty after residents saw in October the danger to contents. Other basements were emptied quickly. As waters rose up Houston Street and into the ground floors of businesses, the Gunter Hotel evacuated guests on horsedrawn buses and moved its lobby offices upstairs. A block away, when the St. Anthony Hotel lost power its employees lit "hundreds of candles" in the lobby, and business went on.[49]

San Antonians began to pick up after the October 1913 flood as sunlight reflected on the rippling waters down St. Mary's Street past the Gunter Hotel, above, and, below, on the new lake east of St. Mary's Street below Travis Street. The Telephone Building is at center and the Central Fire Station at its right.

Utilities were damaged and streetcar service shut down briefly. The only rail line maintaining regular service was the San Antonio, Uvalde & Gulf, which did not serve flood-stricken areas. When several carloads of newsprint destined for the *Express* could not reach San Antonio on the Southern Pacific, the newspaper printed its entire December 6 edition and part of the next day's on the pink newsprint normally reserved for the sports section.[50]

Fortunately, lessons of the October flood were fresh and the city was better prepared. Estimated losses downtown did not exceed $50,000, though bridges in the surrounding county suffered damages totaling a like amount. The only drowning in the city or county was that of a man carried down Leon Creek from Culebra Road.[51]

Afterward came the familiar discussion of building a dam at the end of Olmos Creek or diverting its flow to the west. This time, however, there was an added awareness that outside professional help might be needed. An engineer already working on the city's sewer system, Samuel M. Gray of Providence, Rhode Island, was asked to investigate the river situation and make a report. He submitted a report a month later, acknowledging the problems but concluding that he did not have sufficient data to reach sound conclusions. More study would be needed. Judging from the *Light's* disapproval of Gray's fee of $800, it did not seem likely that the city was going to pay for an in-depth study any time soon.[52]

As the river returned to its banks and residents set about making repairs, George Surkey returned to building the riverbank walls. A temporary work bridge his men built had been washed away, and the stone retaining wall beside St. Mary's College had to be replaced.[53] As the walls neared completion, sod, shrubs, and palm trees joined the cypresses and other trees down the narrow strips between the new channel and high banks to street level.

Modifications were made to the new Commerce Street Bridge to make it more dramatic. With help from Italian-born sculptor Pompeo Coppini, street-level alcoves were added to either side, upgrading the bridge from a plain-

Once the floods ended and the Commerce Street widening and river park projects were completed, a new Commerce Street bridge featured the still-familiar figure of an Indian. A sculpture of the recently-deceased reform mayor Augustus Jones designed by Pompeo Coppini was planned for the opposite alcove on the bridge but was never cast.

SAN ANTONIO

HERBERT BARNARD.

sided span. For benefit of visitors to the river park, Coppini added ornate concrete reliefs to the alcove supports.[54]

To set in the northern alcove, Coppini designed a statue of a seated Augustus Jones to be cast in bronze and placed on a granite pedestal, though it was never cast and the alcove remained empty. For the southern alcove, Coppini's student Waldine Tauch designed in imitation granite a figure of an Indian wearing a headdress and holding in each hand "two fountains of bubbling water," representing the gift of the river below to those who came later. On the alcoves' far corners, cast concrete pilasters tapered upward to the relief of an Indians face. The bridge was lit by streetlight globes at the top of each of the four pilasters.[55]

Nearly 50,000 San Antonians gathered in the streets on the evening of November 21, 1914, for the highlight of the daylong Commerce Street project dedication. The new span was dedicated as Jones Bridge. Celebrants cheered as Mayor Brown recognized River Commissioner George Surkey for his work. The touch of a switch lit up the newly beautified and channeled riverbanks—from Market Street a block south and on north past Commerce Street around the Great Bend and beyond to the Houston Street bridge—with colored lights newly strung across the river, a project of the two-year-old Rotary Club of San Antonio. Rotarians presented the city with twelve pairs of swans to grace the river.[56]

The Chamber of Commerce seized on the new attraction in a 1915 booklet addressed "To you who would escape the rigors of winter with its snow and ice attended by bad colds, danger of pneumonia, and other discomforts." No doubt for the first time in such promotions, an illustration of the Alamo was bumped to the back cover and a drawing of the newly beautified river, in color, filled the front. In making the case that San Antonio "is unlike the average American city of a hundred thousand people," the text plugged the winding river, "its blue waters rippling between banks that are being parked into green esplanades of flowering shrubs and plants."[57]

Momentum for municipal improvement continued, though with mixed results and at a slowing pace. The commission form of city government was adopted, but a city planner was not hired. An irrigation system in San Pedro Park saved its ancient trees, and a new pump started its springs flowing again and raised its lake to the old level. But the city's Boulevard Committee was unsuccessful in getting a San Pedro Boulevard along the banks of the creek.[58]

Nevertheless, the reform movement brought a signal triumph along San Antonio's beloved river— the river park. Businessmen tested its appeal, with tentative results. In 1918 the pre-existing Riverside

Boats gathered at the new Houston Street bridge for an unidentified event, below, about 1916. On the bank immediately to the left, in the basement of the Book Building, four years later the Coffee Shop became the first business at river level.

A balcony was added at the pre-existing Riverside Restaurant in 1918 so diners could overlook the river park.

Restaurant at street level at the southeast corner of the Houston Street bridge came up with the first new commercial construction addressed to the beautified river, a balcony for diners extended partly over the channel for a better view of the newly landscaped banks. On the opposite side of the river, some two years later The Coffee House opened in the basement of the Book Building at the foot of a stairway from the bridge. The Coffee House had its own landing for boats. It was the first business at the river level, and the first of four in an intermittent series in that space during the next three decades until commercial efforts shifted to the riverbanks below the Commerce Street bridge.[59]

Four years after the river park was finished, a visiting writer for *Architectural Record*, I. T. Frary, grasped the essence and import of what had been achieved against so many odds. He filed a perceptive story that appeared, with illustrations, in the magazine's April 1919 issue:

> Few municipalities recognize the possibilities for civic improvement which are to be found in even a small stream of water. Fewer still develop these possibilities when they are recognized.

Occasionally there is a city, however, in which a stream is appreciated and is regarded as something more than part of a drainage system. Among these may be recorded the name of San Antonio, Texas.

To be sure, the stream which San Antonians dignify as a river would be referred to as a creek or brook in a more humid climate, but streams of any size or variety are not sufficiently common in the great Southwest to be trifled with. Even so, the majority of cities would fail to recognize the desirability even of a little stream writhing erratically through the downtown district and withholding from commercial use many acres of valuable real estate.

The average City Council would have built an intercepting sewer, the stream would have disappeared from view and the city would have become as commonplace as any other good hustling, enterprising town.

San Antonio saw further and, tiny and lacking in moisture though her river might be, she decided to make the most of it. She neither condemned it to solitary confinement in a brick sewer nor straightened its course. Instead she let it follow its own sweet way, gave it a wider bed than it demanded, and then made of this bed an attractive little parkway contentedly following the stream's windings and insinuating itself into the most unexpected corners of the downtown district.

Miles of the river still remain undeveloped within the city limits, but in the business center the greatest care has been taken to enhance its attractiveness. No attempt has been made to produce elaborate effects; its banks have been simply grassed over; trees form archways above its course, and flowers here and there brighten it up and add a touch of charm and color, although with but little more of sophistication than nature would employ.

Winding about as it does, it passes under a myriad of bridges, each bridge affording the passersby delightful vistas of fresh, green foliage and quiet waters, a welcome relief from the torrid heat and scorching sun of southern summer days. [60]

The bust of an Indian supporting streetlights, one of four on the corners of the new Commerce Street bridge, faces away from the view of the new river park northward to the Crockett Street bridge. At the sharp bend just beyond, at upper left, a fig tree shades one of the park's newly-planted banks.

3
THE FLOOD OF 1921

Winds gusting up to ninety-five miles an hour lashed the eastern coast of Mexico as the second hurricane of the season hit south of Tampico on September 7, 1921. Inland, as the hurricane swerved sharply north, its intensity lowered to that of a tropical storm, then weakened again. In the night it swung northeastward into Texas near Laredo and headed directly for San Antonio, packing still high winds with violent, heavy thunderstorms.[1]

Hurricane watches were as yet unknown, and San Antonians seemed blissfully unaware that such a storm was heading their way. San Antonians did have a vague idea that something resembling the massive storm of 1819 could happen again, for only nine months earlier a professional flood prevention study had warned that such a disaster "is just as likely to occur next year as at any other time."[2]

Since the two floods of 1913, and a lesser one late the following year, city hall had been dithering over homegrown proposals to address the issue. There was as yet a lack of state and federal funding for such efforts. Finally, in 1920, the city signed on with a top national engineering firm for advice. To

their credit, once they received a report San Antonio officials moved forward with due speed on the study's recommendations.

But the price of the earlier hesitation was the worst cataclysm in San Antonio's history.

Since the floods of 1913, local engineers had steadily advanced ideas for dealing with floodwaters that surged down from Olmos Creek. One engineer recommended slowing them with "a wall pierced by openings" between two low bluffs across the eastern end of Olmos Basin, now the route of Hildebrand Avenue. Another urged digging a channel to send floodwaters around downtown—not westward to Alazan Creek, as proposed in the past, but eastward to Salado Creek. Based "unequivocally upon his record as a drainage engineer," the proposer of this plan dismissed straightening the river channel as "idle talk and out of the question." The channel was "a product of nature," and tampering with it would only make matters worse.[3]

Another engineer, E. A. Giraud, thought that such a channel to Salado Creek was both unnecessary and impractical, since it would require a cut

45

a half-mile deep plus a tunnel more than a mile long. Giraud did agree that straightening the river would be "almost impracticable" financially and would "destroy the natural beauty of the river." He suggested instead "a monolithic concrete dam" between two high bluffs near the mouth of Olmos Basin. Former City Engineer Aaron Pancoast thought this proposal was "the best by far" of any plan yet advanced.[4]

Workmen stand in front of the lumber retaining wall built north of Pecan Street in 1920 in an interim attempt to combat flooding.

While these engineers favored channeling floodwaters near their source, others worried more about fixing specific overflows. Encroachments and obstruc-

tions should be removed, streets raised, bridges made higher so they would not become dams. River Commissioner George Surkey wanted an underground spillway from Navarro Street to Nueva Street to carry overflow beneath downtown. Fire Chief Phil Wright thought there should be two underground spillways, one starting at St. Mary's Street and the other along a northern portion of Navarro Street then known as Romana Street.[5]

Before long, a lull in major floods shifted attention to the other side of the coin—how to deal with the problems of less water. Erosion was silting the channel above the river park. In the absence of heavy rains, the channel had to be flushed out again with fire hoses. The city engineer, Norwegian immigrant Hans R. F. Helland, thought silting from erosion could be stopped by lining the banks for the five blocks from Navarro Street to Houston Street with twenty-two-foot-high retaining walls of pine planks with cypress pilings. Suction pumps could remove whatever silt made it into the channel. Parks and Sanitation Commissioner Ray Lambert agreed, adding that climbing vines could turn those walls into "an object of beauty." But bids in 1917 came in too high, and the plan was scrapped.[6]

Two years later, several flood issues were addressed in a successful, wide-ranging bond issue that included $200,000 for "widening, deepening, altering and changing" the river channel to prevent flooding. Lumber walls were built the next year along the winding one-block segment between Travis and Pecan streets. Other funds authorized new bridges plus a straight channel to eliminate the convoluted bend at the northern edge of downtown, permitting construction of the long-awaited Municipal Auditorium on the site of the bend.[7]

Lumber walls and a straighter channel would reduce some problems, but city commissioners finally had to give in to the realization that they alone could not sort through the surfeit of proposals, counterproposals, and random projects and half-projects to cure the dangers of major flooding. It was time to call in experts from out of town. On June 9, 1920, the city signed on with the nationally recognized Boston firm Metcalf & Eddy. Partner Leonard Metcalf was a native of Galveston and knew San Antonio well, having done four technical reports for the San Antonio Water Works Company.

Engineers led by Metcalf and an associate, Charles W. Sherman, spent nearly six months studying local conditions and meeting with officials from Mayor Sam C. Bell to River Engineer Albert Marbach to Citizens Flood Prevention Committee President L. J. Hart. City data on the river and its tributaries was considered "too limited to enable safe conclusions," so the engineers pored over U.S. Weather Bureau and U.S. Geological Survey data. They walked "practically

every foot" of the river through the city as well as the length of San Pedro Creek, and explored the usually dry drainage basins of Alazan, Martinez, and Apache creeks.[8]

On December 6, 1920, Metcalf & Eddy presented city commissioners with a 348-page report. There were thirty tables of data and sixty diagrams, drawings, and maps. Maintenance may have become more regular, and the lumber retaining walls would help, but the basic problems remained: the narrow width of the river, lack of a dam, and riverbed obstructions. Measures already taken would not prevent another flood like that of December 1913, which sent 6,000 cubic feet of water per second through downtown. The greater danger was a hundred-year flood like that of 1819, which could deliver a brutal 22,000 cubic feet or more per second.[9]

The Boston engineers concluded that building a new channel to carry floodwaters through downtown was impractical and unnecessary. Instead, the existing channel could be improved by eliminating six bends, shortening the river by more than a mile and a half and increasing its capacity to 12,000 cubic feet per second, twice the volume of the second 1913 flood. The remaining waters of a hundred-year flood could be held back in the retaining basin of a dam between

Galveston native Leonard Metcalf headed the Boston engineering firm of Metcalf & Eddy, hired by San Antonio in 1920 to come up with a broad plan to prevent flooding.

the high bluffs near the mouth of Olmos Creek.[10]

Contrary to common belief, Metcalf & Eddy did not recommend a cutoff channel to eliminate the Great Bend, either above or below ground. The Citizens Flood Prevention Committee did give the engineers Willard Simpson's 1911 report recommending such a cutoff, which would allow the bend to be filled in and developed. The Boston engineers at first agreed with Simpson's proposal, but by the time they finished their report in December 1920 they had concluded that such a conduit would be inadequate during hundred-year floods and was not cost effective.[11]

Rather than eliminating the Great Bend, Metcalf & Eddy recommended simply deepening the entire channel, including the bend. The channel was to be a standard width of seventy feet, flanked by steep masonry walls and grassy banks. Although engineers acknowledged the appeal of landscaping, they recommended eliminating all shrubs and trees, which "not only tend to arrest the current but also, by catching sand and gravel, to make barriers and shoals in the stream."[12]

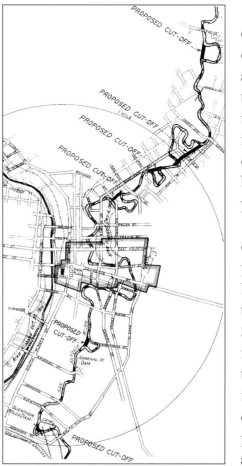

Cost of the entire project was estimated at $4 million. City officials swallowed hard. But they adopted the report, making clear that raising such an amount immediately "would be impossible in the light of other urgent needs of the city." It could, however, be stretched over ten or twenty years.[13]

City officials began working on the proposals even before the plan was formally presented. In November 1920 they began negotiations with C. H. Guenther & Son's Pioneer Flour Mills on the report's top priority, widening the constricted channel across from the U.S. Arsenal south of downtown by removing both the picturesque wooden upper mill and its dam. In March the city advertised for bids on another high priority, eliminating the twisting bend on the future site of Municipal Auditorium.[14]

By then it was spring, and the 1921 fiesta was approaching. The Fiesta de San Jacinto Association made its usual request for a permit to decorate trees along the river. This time the city replied that, since all trees along the banks were going to be cut down to

clear the channel, there would be "nothing to decorate but the walls." The permit was denied.[15]

The sudden realization that the river park's carefully planted trees and shrubs were about to be cleared hit San Antonio like a bombshell.

On March 31, 1921, a wave of protest swept the city, from "men and women in all walks of life." Mayor Sam Bell and Parks Commissioner Ray Lambert were besieged with irate visitors and indignant phone calls. "It would be a disaster to take away the trees from the banks of the San Antonio River," one protester told the *Express*. "Nothing short of a calamity," said another. Declared a third: "I think that the man who would lift an ax to remove the beautiful old trees and landmarks along the San Antonio River should be ostracized from the community."

When Lambert was summoned to address a public meeting on the subject at the Woman's Club

the next afternoon, the mayor and the parks commissioner hastily announced that they had decided not to remove the trees after all.[16]

The Boston engineers had emphasized that a flood control project should start at once: "We doubt if the citizens realize the ruinous loss which would result today, with the present condition of the river channels, from such a flood as that of a century ago. When such a flood will recur, no man can say." But since such floods generally occur on an average of once every hundred years, and since it had already been a hundred years since the last such flood in San Antonio, "a very great flood ought to be expected in the near future," they warned. "This disastrous flood is just as likely to occur next year as at any other time."[17]

Nine months after that report was issued, the remains of the season's second hurricane zeroed in on San Antonio.

Prior to the evening of September 9, the river north of the Houston Street bridge, left, flowed peacefully through the river park. A deluge in the night was still sending a torrent down the channel at 6:30 the next morning, right. The high water mark several feet above the railing left a smear visible on the white wall at right of center.

Advance showers on the night of Thursday, September 8, 1921, broke a dry spell of two months. San Antonio's parched earth absorbed most of the first rainfall. Occasional hard showers followed early the next day.[18]

The main body of the storm hit Friday afternoon. Severe thunderstorms broke out at 6 p.m. "Lightning flashed almost continuously, and the thunder boomed and reverberated throughout the heavens," reported the *Light*. After three hours the thunderstorms ended and the rain's intensity began to ebb. The river was four feet from the top of the plank retaining wall near Pecan Street, but residents went to bed thinking all was well. Those who stayed awake expected to see at the most another flood like those in 1913.[19]

Rain over Olmos Creek's watershed, however, had been twice as heavy as that over San Antonio. At 9 p.m. Olmos Creek began to overflow its banks.

As its waters surged into the San Antonio River, the river began rising one foot every five minutes in Brackenridge Park, causing more than 100 tourist campers to scurry for higher ground.

At 11:30 p.m., waters from the Olmos reached the Fourth Street/Lexington Avenue Bridge, at the northern edge of downtown, where the river was already two feet above its banks. An hour later, water there was up nearly three feet more.[20]

At midnight Saturday, September 10, the river went over its banks onto St. Mary's Street and within twelve minutes was more than six feet deep at the Travis Street intersection as six north-south streets turned into auxiliary river channels. At St. Mary's and Houston streets, water reached nearly to the mezzanine of the Gunter Hotel. Floodwaters drowned the boiler fires of the well pumps at the waterworks on Market Street at 12:30 a.m., shutting off most of the

One bridge destroyed by the impact of debris was that at Fourth Street/Lexington Avenue, left. Debris simply backed up at the concrete Commerce Street bridge, far right, shown as receding water revealed tops of trees along the banks.

city's water supply. An hour later, water topped the walls of the city's power plant beside the river on Villita Street. Workers threw the switches, shutting off the city's electricity. Then the telephone system went down. Telegraph lines went out. The *Light's* Associated Press wire still functioned, allowing news to come in and be sent out. Otherwise, San Antonio was cut off from the rest of the world.[21]

Quantities of oil—much of it stored in open vats and tanks by the two breweries and waterworks pump houses—were flushed downstream, swirling on the surface and leaving smears marking high water points on buildings. Making floodwaters even more dangerous was the mass of floating debris—bedsprings, automobiles, furniture, splintered lumber, washtubs, pianos. Some refuse jammed behind bridge trusses, creating dams that made waters even higher.[22]

Some basement floors downtown buckled from water seeping up through the ground. As plate glass windows burst, water rushed in to meet floodwaters already rising from basements. A stack of rugs and furniture was swept across Main Avenue from Stowers Furniture Company showrooms, and lunch counters and food supplies were pushed into soggy, oil-stained, disordered piles at the backs of the Saratoga and Metropolitan restaurants.[23]

Screams and cries echoed in the darkness across the floodwaters, as police and firemen attempted rescues. City officials put in a distress call to Maj. Gen. John M. Hines, commander of the U.S. Army's Second Division at Camp Travis, beside Fort Sam Houston. By midnight, hundreds of khaki-clad soldiers of the Second Engineers, First and Twentieth Infantry regiments and Twelfth and Fifteenth Field

Nearly 2,000 soldiers from nearby Fort Sam Houston arrived in the city as the flood worsened in the early hours of Saturday morning. By daybreak soldiers were guarding the city's main intersection of Houston and St. Mary's streets, already on horseback, far left, and patrolling in pontoon boats.

Artillery units were arriving on the scene. Army trucks rumbled to a stop and troops leapt out, formed in columns of twos, and headed for flooded areas. Cavalrymen plunged into the water on horseback to reach victims.[24]

At least 500 rescues were made, lit by flashlights, smoky kerosene lanterns, and automobile headlights. In a backyard on King William Street, one woman made it to the roof of an outbuilding and shouted for help for three hours until rescuers arrived. A twelve-year-old boy clung to a tree on South Flores Street with a five-year-old on his shoulders until both were rescued.

Others were on their own. The howling of their fox terrier awakened the Harry Liecks, who found their two-year-old in a bed floating on a rear sleeping porch. The family headed upstairs. On Fourth Street,

a man barely escaped from his apartment as part of the house was swept into the river. His wife and child were nowhere to be seen. Searching downstream, an hour later he heard cries from remains of a house lodged against a railing of the Navarro Street bridge. He broke through the roof to find his missing wife and child safe on a mattress floating within one foot of the ceiling.[25]

Residential areas hardest hit were the poor neighborhoods beside San Pedro Creek and Alazan Creek and its tributaries, Apache and Martinez creeks, in western San Antonio. Alazan Creek went down a relatively steep grade, making its flow all the more forceful as the Alazan and its tributaries flooded simultaneously. Dozens of homes were carried away. One family in the 1000 block of Nogalitos Street believed that the safest place was inside their small

Downtown traffic began to struggle past the Gunter Hotel on the morning of September 10, left, as others dealt with the consequences of living in homes, right, within the river's floodplain.

home. Would-be rescuers scattered as a wall of water came crashing down, sweeping two small boys and a young girl outside the house, never to be seen again. Initial casualty estimates ran as high as 250.[26]

The crest came about 2 a.m., some three hours after the storm had moved on and ended twenty-three hours of steady rainfall. Nearly seven inches of rain had fallen on the city. The Olmos Creek drainage area got as many as fourteen inches. As the river crested downtown, a thousand acres of the city were inundated. A three-quarter-square-mile area of downtown was under two to twelve feet of water. Military engineers estimated the velocity of floodwaters at 22,000 cubic feet per second, the precise flow engineers had predicted for such a flood nine months earlier.[27]

As the storm headed northeast past Austin it met a high-pressure area backing in from East Texas. The storm intensified and abruptly dissipated near Taylor, leaving that town reeling beneath 23.11 inches of rain, the largest twenty-four-hour rainfall yet recorded in the United States. Unofficial reports indicated thirty-six inches fell during the same period in nearby Thrall.[28]

As dawn broke over San Antonio, receding waters revealed a frightful scene. Pictures snapped after the 1913 floods show smiling residents wading or dunking themselves in floodwaters, carriages surging onward, streetcars throwing up spray as they rolled forward. This time, stunned San Antonians picked their way carefully along debris-strewn streets, stripped of wooden paving blocks, and gazed soberly at the destruction. Others stood in food lines awaiting breakfast. A few spectators gamely tried to grin beside canoes they held upright in the receding water, but

As the morning wore on, water in the northern Great Bend was down to the level of Crockett Street, shown at left looking east. The view at right, looking in the opposite direction, shows a soldier guarding the scene as the river receded further.

Floodwaters left a high water mark on the main building of St. Mary's College, top left, now the Omni La Mansion del Rio, and required priests at the adjacent St. Mary's Catholic Church, top right, to remove pews and hang vestments out to dry. Only a tree kept the Ford at lower left from being swept into the river, according to a notation on the back of the photo. Windows at the Citizens Auto Company were caved in by floodwaters, though damage decreased as Travis Street, a sea of mud, gradually rose higher past Travis Park Methodist Church and the Saint Anthony Hotel.

Interiors of stores and offices were turned into sodden masses of furniture, goods, and files, as shown at the start of cleanup efforts at the Bell Jewelry Company, upper left, two doors from the river on Commerce Street. Bridges were especially hard-hit. At top right, stunned San Antonians gathered at the St. Mary's Street bridge past piles of paving blocks and an overturned auto beside the Oblate Fathers Home next to St. Mary's Church. One of the oddest victims of the flood was a model of the enormous proposed Alamo monument designed by Alfred Giles, lower right, that stood beside the northern Navarro Street bridge until removed when the destroyed bridge was replaced. Flooding also destroyed the rail bridge, lower left, into the Pioneer Flour Mills plant south of downtown.

the more dominant images are of soldiers paddling in pontoon boats patrolling downtown streets.

As many as 1,500 soldiers were at first dismissed to return to their posts. Then looters were discovered picking through department stores and office buildings, whose doors were torn off and street windows shattered, the merchandise jumbled and washed into mud-smeared heaps. The soldiers, called back to duty, spread through flooded areas, made several arrests, and kept looting from becoming widespread. A civilian shot by a soldier on guard duty in front of a store on South Santa Rosa Street later died of his wounds.[29]

Newspapers provided San Antonians with their first general accounts of the tragedy. Water at the *Express* building, beside the river at Commerce and Crockett streets, had quickly filled the basement pressroom and reached the first floor just past midnight, so the paper missed its Saturday morning edition. Publisher Charles Diehl's fiercely competi-

tive afternoon *Light*, on Travis Street, was on higher ground, though its basement pressroom also flooded. The *Light* put out a makeshift extra edition on a press used for printing menus at the St. Anthony Hotel two blocks away, and managed to get out a regular edition that afternoon.[30]

Early damage estimates were as high as $10 million, though a more sober estimate made later by the U.S. Army Corps of Engineers at Fort Sam Houston put the total at $3.7 million. Confirmed deaths ended up at fifty-one, all but four of them along the San Pedro and Alazan creek systems. One grave at San Fernando Cemetery was dug large enough to hold a family of six. In addition to those known dead, another twenty-three persons were listed as missing. The true total was no doubt higher, considering families like those of Mariano Escobedo.[31]

Escobedo, a laborer, left his small home on the banks of Alazan Creek near El Paso Street a few days before the flood, in search of work. He had reached

West Texas when he heard of the disaster. Without steady work he did not have enough money to return immediately, and those whom he asked for help did not believe his story of wanting to check on his family. But Escobedo gradually worked his way back. He arrived in San Antonio the first week in October to find his home gone and no sign of his wife or their two young children. The Red Cross had no record of them among the dead or missing. Escobedo searched for days, without results. Police suspected they had not learned of many others also washed away.[32]

The rescues over, workers began helping the homeless and displaced. On the first day more than 2,000 persons were aided by local American Red Cross workers, headquartered in the second-floor auditorium of the Market House on Milam Park. By the second day of relief efforts, the Red Cross esti-mated it had made nearly 25,000 sandwiches at the Market House—"all containing meat of some kind"— and dispensed them to shelters throughout the city. San Antonio women volunteers under the leadership of Hannah Hirschberg used 100 automobiles to take Red Cross food and clothing to those who could not come to shelters. Cash contributions were distributed once applicants for aid were verified, "principally by women's clubs, pastors, and priests."[33]

Military efforts, directed by Col. B. A. Poore, were based near the Alamo at the YMCA on Avenue E, where soldiers bunked. There another 10,000 sandwiches and a like number of cups of hot coffee were made and served by women from San Antonio's Protestant churches. Meals were served at field kitchens in a vacant lot across the street. Soldiers strung makeshift telephone lines so relief efforts could be coordinated

Only the International & Great Northern tracks stopped the ruins of the building at left from being carried further by Alazan Creek floodwaters. Soldiers and volunteer workers soon had food distribution lines set up in the stricken neighborhood.

As relief efforts got under way, a pump at top left took water out of the basement of the National Bank of Commerce on Main Plaza. At top right, soldiers began stringing up telephone wires near the courthouse to restore some sort of communication for rescue workers. At right, trucks dumped wooden paving blocks scooped from downtown streets by floodwaters.

and served meals from mobile field kitchens spread through the Alazan Creek area. Tents and cots were distributed to the homeless.[34]

Some 600 civilians under the chairmanship of Albert Steves Jr. canvassed the city for clothing. A Chamber of Commerce businessmen's relief committee took charge of checking reports of those dead, injured, and missing. Its chairman, Sylvan Lang, was confident that a $25,000 fund drive would be completed by noon Monday, September 12. Other groups—the Salvation Army, Elks, Shriners—were also assisting. New Braunfels textile magnate Harry Landa sent down two trucks carrying 450 loaves of bread as aid began to arrive from outside the city.[35]

But help from outsiders was not exactly welcome.

"San Antonio is able to take care of herself," declared Mayor O. B. Black, who was declining offers of aid from cities throughout Texas. He also rejected a group of doctors and nurses offered by the state health officer. The mayor was particularly definite about not welcoming unemployed workers, who were beginning to arrive in search of work. The city's first duty, he declared, was to offer work to the city's own unemployed.[36]

Within two days of the flood, a semblance of public utilities had returned. Electricity was restored to most nonflooded areas, telephone service to a fourth of the city. Two dozen streetcar crewmen used their own automobiles to carry passengers, free of charge, along streetcar lines still without power, and were reimbursed for gasoline by the Public Service Company. Even though city water pumps were not functioning, the force of newly energized artesian wells and springs had maintained a low water pressure through

Soldiers from Fort Sam Houston and other volunteers set up food lines that served more than 20,000 hot meals after the 1921 flood. The Fox Company, a film processor, used the tools of its trade to send customers postcards graphically explaining why their orders were delayed.

much of the city. By Monday, September 12, pumping had resumed to parts of the city where mains were undamaged. Sounds of chugging engines pumping out basements and the clattering cleanup of mud and debris were everywhere.[37]

The main downtown business district stayed closed for more than a week as debris was cleared with the aid of more than 120 trucks, half of them compliments of the U.S. Army and others rented by the city from the Texas Highway Department. Contractors put workers on three eight-hour shifts daily until the major Houston, Travis, and St. Mary's street arteries were repaved. Nine days after the flood, on September 19, the last soldiers guarding the main business district were sent back to Camp Travis. Except for two blocks hard to access because of damaged bridges, the district reopened that night. "Immense crowds" thronged in to view the progress and to shop.[38]

Nine days after the flood ended, soldiers packed their boats and supplies and headed back to Fort Sam Houston.

When emergency food distribution ended two days later, relief workers had filled 6,770 grocery orders and served more than 20,600 hot meals, 57,200 sandwiches, and countless cups of coffee.[39]

Salvaged lumber and building materials were distributed among the homeless, and businessmen rushed to recover by selling damaged goods to raise cash. On the sidewalk in front of his store at Houston Street and Main Avenue, Nathan Sinkin spread out boxes of damaged merchandise for sale at 20 to 25 cents. Winerich Motor Sales offered soldiers "slightly flood damaged" Overlands for $625, accompanied by ninety-day guarantees.[40] San Fernando Cathedral dedicated its new main altar of Carrara marble with gold mosaic inlay to the memory of San Antonio victims of both World War I and the recent flood.[41]

There remained an awareness that things could have been much worse. Had the rainfall been as heavy as it became soon after over Bell, Milam, and Williamson counties, engineers concluded that "the destruction at San Antonio would have been so great as to make that actually suffered there seem insignificant."[42]

In far southern San Antonio, the cresting of Alazan and Apache creeks at different times before they joined San Pedro Creek and then the San Antonio River kept waters at a fairly steady level past Mission Concepción. The high waters had passed before the highest floodwaters began moving south from downtown. Progress of those floodwaters had been slowed when the wall of downtown buildings acted as a barrier, allowing more water to be absorbed into the ground while more was diverted into basements. Because of all this, the river in far southern San Antonio "overflowed its banks only slightly."[43]

Mayor Black's rigid dependence on self-help reflected a pre–New Deal era of self-reliance that made federal aid programs rare. It should be noted, however, that though San Antonio may have recovered from the flood without any direct help from state or federal governments, the mayor's bravado was made easier thanks to assistance from San Antonio–based but federally funded Army troops and their trucks for the cleanup.

In mid-October, U.S. Secretary of Commerce Herbert Hoover wrote San Antonio Chamber of Commerce President Morris Stern to declare that, according to the *Express*, the city's achievement "without accepting one dollar of aid from outside was one of the finest examples of cooperation and civic spirit of which he knew." Hoover congratulated the city and wished to assure its residents that "they had won the admiration of the nation."[44]

San Antonians would have to be satisfied with only the nation's admiration again in the years ahead, as they taxed themselves in a series of bond issues to prevent future flooding.

There was one positive implication from it all. Had the flood of 1921 not occurred, canny observers wondered how serious city officials—who were already beginning to suggest a timeline of up to twenty years—would have remained about imple-

menting all of the recommended flood prevention measures. After the flood, Metcalf & Eddy's Charles Sherman, who had worked closely with city officials on the study and sensed their reactions, revealed himself as one of those skeptics.

An Army cartoonist at Fort Sam Houston's Camp Travis linked the Second Division's World War I victories at Saint Mihiel and Chateau Thierry in France a few years earlier with the troops' successful service during the San Antonio Flood of 1921.

In preparing their study, engineers were quite pleased that fragmentary accounts of the enormous flood in 1819 had survived to give them a benchmark against which to measure future major floods. Sherman feared that since the lesser floods of 1913 were "so much in excess of any flood within the memory of the people of San Antonio," the city would conclude that efforts to prevent such floods as those would be adequate. Metcalf & Eddy recommendations would be scaled back, a key dam would not be built, and San Antonio would be left without adequate protection.[45]

The unprecedented trauma from the flood of 1921, however, virtually guaranteed that San Antonians would become quite serious about taming even the worst floodwaters.

That flood control along the river downtown eventually would yield other enormous benefits, already imagined but hardly expected.

4
TAMING THE RIVER
AND THE GREAT BEND

San Antonio was functioning again as a city within two weeks after the record waters of September 10, 1921, receded. Train service had resumed, utilities were restored, stores were open, the homeless were sheltered, and emergency relief efforts had ended. It was time to deal with the future.

City hall had in hand a road map to flood remedies laid out by some of the nation's finest civil engineers. But there were going to have to be adjustments. How to cope with high water around the Great Bend when so many citizens kept raising beautification issues bedeviled city officials for another eight years, and the dynamics of the solution confuses some analysts to this day. But straightening most of the lesser bends was not a political problem. And the biggest recommendation, building a dam at the mouth of Olmos Creek, debated for nearly a century, at last seemed a certainty.

The coming decade would be a melee of scores and fouls personal and technical, with cheers and catcalls from the sidelines. Fast-moving adversaries swerved deceptively through the opposition to sink a long shot, only to have the achievement sometimes recalled and cancelled. Some players were ejected permanently; others nursed their pride on the sidelines and got back in. In hindsight, so many of the individual plays developed or prepared the way for some unique, now irreplaceable facet of the scene that it becomes clear what a major victory the final score was for the future of the San Antonio River.

At the beginning, a world still thinking of San Antonio as a disaster zone to be avoided had to get a message like that delivered by the San Antonio Real Estate Board at a mid-October 1921 real estate convention luncheon in Fort Worth: "The flood is over and San Antonio is at work."[1] Contractors indeed had resumed construction of the latest additions to the skyline—the Maverick Building on Houston Street and the Frost National Bank Building on Main Plaza.

Lingering handicaps had to be dealt with. Notably, in a city of bridges, thirteen of twenty-seven spans were rendered unusable by the flood and needed

The dam of the upper Guenther Mill south of downtown was dynamited in 1926 during a major flood control effort to clear and straighten the river channel. Across the river are buildings of the U.S. Arsenal, since restored as corporate headquarters of H-E-B.

quick repairs or replacements. One, the 1890 "Letters of Gold" iron bridge on St. Mary's Street, was replaced and then reassembled across the river in Brackenridge Park. Most vexing was the loss of two key bridges on Navarro Street, which snarled traffic in the southwestern central business district.[2]

A temporary wooden bridge was thrown up in place of the wrecked Navarro Street bridge across the northern leg of the Great Bend at Crockett Street. Once another wooden bridge could be finished a block east on North Presa Street, to detour traffic, the bridge at Navarro and Crockett could be replaced with a permanent one. The second wrecked Navarro Street bridge was three blocks farther south, across the southern leg of the Great Bend and known as the Mill Bridge for its proximity to the old Lewis Mill.[3]

Bridges of arched concrete were already planned to replace the two Navarro Street bridges, having been funded by the bond issue of 1919. Despite the urgency

after the flood, there were long delays. First, bids came in high. Plans for the shorter bridge, the ninety-eight-foot span at Crockett Street, were switched to the more economical steel, and new bids were taken. After further holdups caused by wet weather and slow shipments, the bridge at Navarro and Crockett was finally completed in December 1922.

Work was still winding up on the Mill Bridge, its two steel spans with overhead trusses having come down only six months before. The new, elegantly detailed Mill Bridge, twice as wide as its predecessor and featuring three graceful concrete arches, opened early in 1923. It has been a favorite of photographers ever since.[4]

In addition to the bridges, other landmarks suffered damage in varying degrees. Several dozen vintage adobe homes on side streets collapsed, as their predecessors had in the flood of 1819, and had to be cleared away. The biggest loss was the 1857 stone St. Mary's Catholic Church on St. Mary's Street near the river, designed by San Antonio's noted mid-nineteenth-century architect, John Fries, and considered easier to replace with a larger building than to repair.[5]

As leftover business from the flood was tidied up and daily lives became more orderly, the cacophony of demands for a permanent

Nearly a year and a half after the flood of 1921, engineers were finally able to replace the damaged Mill Bridge on southern Navarro Street was this graceful span, also designated Mill Bridge.

remedy had to be faced. Realizing at last the full power of an unchecked river to destroy their city, San Antonians emerged from every sector to make known their hopes and fears. Lower-income residents of western San Antonio suspected that problems on Alazan Creek would be ignored in favor of channel improvements in the business district. Southern San Antonians feared their channel would not be widened, and that floodwaters would rush through a straightened channel upstream and be dumped on the south side. Some businessmen believed that advocates of beautification were more concerned with pretty landscaping than with the danger of floods and had no appreciation of the cash value of riverbed land. Women's organizations suspected those businessmen of being in cahoots with politicians to make a few dollars.

In spite of all these concerns, a public meeting did reflect consensus for a dam on Olmos Creek.[6]

The chief of the U.S. Army Corps of Engineers unit based at Fort Sam Houston, Col. Edgar Jadwin, made a survey at the direction of his superiors in Washington. Jadwin's engineers mapped the Olmos Creek valley and found Metcalf & Eddy engineers' test borings for a dam to be in an ideal location. Jadwin recommended an earthen dam, but a local civilian engineer, Clinton Kearney, dispatched by Mayor O. B. Black on a visual reconnaissance, thought the dam should be of concrete. Whatever the ultimate material, Jadwin made clear to the city that Washington would have no part in financing a dam.[7]

Federal purse strings to relieve suffering from such disasters would not loosen for another six years, after the nation's worst natural disaster up to the New Orleans flood of 2005, the flooding along the Mississippi River in 1927 that left more than one million people homeless. Local financing did not always provide the supervision or expertise that outside authorities could offer. This led, as in San Antonio, to uncertainty and expensive changes while a project was under way and sometimes to basic flaws in the final product, left for correction by future generations.

In 1925 the "Letters of Gold" bridge over the river on South St. Mary's Street was disassembled and reconstructed, left, across the river in Brackenridge Park, where it remains.

In tune with the sentiment of the times, Mayor Black played the self-reliance card once again. He outlined three methods of financing available to San Antonio in 1921: state aid, city aid, and improvement districts. He came down heavy against state aid. To accept it "would be in violation of the self-help so far evinced by the city," Black declared. "It would never do."

After the chest thumping, Black admitted that state aid could not even be requested for a year or more, since the legislature was not in session and then would require a two-thirds majority vote, to say nothing of other limitations. Less problematic were improvement districts, in which residents could vote to tax themselves. City funding would require charter changes and approval of a majority of citizens. That turned out to be the chosen route, though the process would be long. Reports had to be made and approved, and a bond issue vote had to authorize funding before contractors could be selected and actual work could begin.[8]

It took nearly three years for plans to be worked out and for citizens to approve $2.8 million in bonds to pay for it. Then came the question of who would supervise the work. Boston's Metcalf & Eddy had done a thorough study, but its engineers' insistence that riverbank trees and shrubbery be removed had displeased those who worked so many years for an attractive river. Many businessmen, too, were no doubt irked at rejection of their plan for an underground conduit bypassing the Great Bend so it could be filled in for development, and may have hoped for more influence with local engineers. Edwin P. Arneson, speaking on behalf of the San Antonio chapter of the American Association of Engineers, appealed "for the employment of San Antonio engineers exclusively on the project."[9]

So it was no surprise when a San Antonio–based engineer, Samuel F. Crecelius, was picked to plan the $1.5 million Olmos Dam project. Crecelius, a retired colonel in the U.S. Army Corps of Engineers, had designed two dams near Laredo and directed dam and navigation projects in Missouri, Indiana, West Virginia, and Kentucky. He went to work at once.[10]

Visiting members of the U.S. Army Corps of Engineers were given a tour of the Olmos Dam construction site by Samuel Crecelius, in civilian dress, who was directing the project for the city of San Antonio.

Olmos Dam was completed in 1926 to prevent floodwaters from surging into San Antonio. Across the top was a roadway, lit by a series of covered lights atop the railings. It was rerouted below the dam and replaced by a spillway in the 1970s.

In two years work was finished on Olmos Dam, a concrete wonder 80 feet high and 1,925 feet long. Behind the dam stretched a newly purchased retaining basin of 1,100 acres, where a park and golf course were planned. Across the top, a roadway at last linked the nearby San Antonio neighborhood of Laurel Heights with the small city of Alamo Heights, incorporated five years before. At dedication ceremonies on December 11, 1926, a cavalcade of automobiles led by San Antonio Mayor John W. Tobin drove from the San Antonio side to meet cars from Alamo Heights midway. Tobin shook hands with Alamo Heights Mayor Pro Tem W. H. Hume, substituting for the crusty Mayor Robert O'Grady, who had gone deer hunting.[11]

While dam construction was going on, in the fall of 1924 a crew began to clear, straighten and widen Alazan Creek where it joined San Pedro Creek and, just beyond, to do the same where San Pedro Creek joined the river near Mission Concepción, two miles south of downtown. In the river channel to the south, in January 1926 a steam shovel moved into place and in six months dug a 445-foot cutoff channel, eliminating a bend that had meandered 2,100 feet. The old riverbed was added to the new Concepción Park.[12]

Next to go were two smaller bends in the southern river channel, one above the new park and the other at Pioneer Flour Mills, where a new 300-foot-wide cut smoothed and shortened a sharp switchback on the 1,200-foot bend. Across from the U.S. Arsenal just upstream, the old Guenther Upper Mill and its dam were removed to straighten and widen the channel.[13]

Two large bends were taken out at opposite ends of downtown. One was what remained of the Bowen's Island S-shaped bend, where the Great Bend flowed west almost to the Bexar County courthouse before doubling back east and then heading south. To the north, replacing a twisting 1,830-foot double bend with a straight channel cleared the site for Municipal Auditorium and raised the issue of beautification in a section of the river just north of the river park.[14]

Property owners suggested that a fountain ten feet in diameter be in the middle of the new riverbed west of the auditorium. An operator could make spray from five concentric rings rise twenty-five feet. Six colored searchlights below the water line could evoke anything from "a waving field of ripening wheat to a crimson pyramid many feet high that looks like a huge bonfire."

Mayor Tobin, an accomplished politician, saw a parade coming and got in front of it. As for a fountain near the auditorium, Tobin said he liked the idea so much that there should be five more fountains, all visible from key downtown intersections. When the city prepared to replace strings of lights washed away by the flood and to pay for the electricity, Tobin declared: "The river is one of San Antonio's real assets, and we are to develop plans that will make it a thing of real beauty and something visitors will remember and comment on long after they leave the city."[15]

By this time the San Antonio Conservation Society, recently organized in an ultimately futile effort to save the city's 1859 Market House, had segued into stressing the importance of preserving the city's natural beauty. In September 1924, members presented city council with a puppet show written by the society's first president, Emily Edwards, entitled "The Goose

The sharp bend below Pioneer Flour Mills, left, was shortened slightly during river straightening in the 1920s. A larger project was construction of the Great Bend cutoff channel, below right, that also lopped off two curves that helped form what was once known as Bowen's Island.

That Laid the Golden Eggs." The puppets, some designed to resemble council members, debated the importance of preserving the city's unique aspects. Two months later, society members had the idea of giving city officials a boat ride. An immediate goal was to show how preservation of the river's beauty was a fine reason to change the next spring fiesta's Battle of Flowers Parade into a river parade.[16]

Only two council members showed up—Mayor Tobin and Ray Lambert, who was also the parks commissioner. In one of the four rowboats was the newly hired flood control engineer, Samuel Crecelius. In another was society stalwart Margaret Lewis, also president of the parade-sponsoring Battle of Flowers Association. The tour left a landing at Ninth Street and two hours later stopped at Market Street, on the Great Bend. Spectators, recruited to station themselves on bridges along the route, cheered as the boats passed.

As the flotilla approached a large cottonwood tree near the Houston Street bridge, Colonel Crecelius declared to Emily Edwards that anything blocking the river channel would be taken out. Recalled Edwards, "That [tree] was so near it . . . I said, 'Would that have to go?' And he said, 'Oh, yes, that would have to go.' And so I turned to Mrs. Lewis [in the next boat] and I said, 'Mrs. Lewis, that has to go.' And Mrs. Lewis said—she was very excitable–'That does NOT have to go!' And [her] boat began to rock."

Mrs. Lewis's fellow passenger, Ray Lambert, was "a great big man." No doubt clutching the sides of his rocking boat, he quickly replied, "No, no, no!"

The tree did not go. Emily Edwards said saving that cottonwood tree was the first victory of the San Antonio Conservation Society.[17]

In 1926 the city strung lights across the river park between Navarro and St. Mary's streets to replace those lost during the flood.

The next fiesta parade was not held on the river, but the new flood engineer did have a quick lesson in what he was up against. Paving the Great Bend over, even just clearing away trees, was obviously still out of the question. The wrangle would last five years and cost Crecelius his job. An outside engineering firm would be hired and fired as well. To accommodate one mistaken calculation, a penny-pinching city hall would have to endure the embarrassment of chopping off the rear of the police headquarters it had just built beside the river, leaving scars on side walls that can still be seen. Developers would be thwarted again and again in their efforts to slip by some affront to the integrity of the Great Bend.

Things started out smoothly enough. To placate both those who would deepen the Great Bend for flood control and remove its foliage and those wishing to preserve its natural beauty, Crecelius came up with a compromise. He proposed two adjacent 650-foot-long underground box culverts, but as a shortcut for overflow only. When floodwaters came, a gate at the bend's entrance would be lowered to keep floodwaters out and divert them into the new channel. At all other times the river would continue as usual around the bend, which, no longer endangered by flood overflow, would not have to be deepened nor be stripped of trees and shrubs.[18] The concept became a crucial element in developing the future River Walk.

Paying for the compromise was the next problem. Most of the 1924 flood prevention bond funds had been used up, and another $1 million would have to be approved. At Mayor Tobin's insistence, Crecelius cut right-of-way costs by narrowing the parallel culverts' total width from seventy feet to fifty. If their

walls were made strong enough, they could also support eight-story buildings with valuable frontage on Commerce, Market, and Dolorosa streets. Renting frontage for the buildings could bring the city a quick $200,000 to put back into flood control.[19]

But Mayor Tobin was ailing and having an extended convalescence in San Diego, California. While there, he was elected to a second term in absentia. In his absence, Crecelius's plan ran into opposition. One faction thought a new street should go above the culverts, not new buildings. Crecelius replied that such an idea had been "definitely abandoned." He was promptly countermanded by Acting Mayor Phil Wright, who announced that the street would indeed be built. Wright added that a public restroom building would go up in the new space north of Commerce Street for the benefit of shoppers. From San Diego, Mayor Tobin sent a sketch showing how the structure could also include a barbershop plus a Turkish bath.[20]

As construction began on the southern section of the twin culverts and right-of-way acquisition proceedings continued for the northern section, the off-again, on-again street was suddenly off again. This time, businessmen rebelled against the culverts' channel being narrowed, and petitioned to return the width to seventy feet. Water from a cloudburst north of the new dam might be held back, they said, but a cloudburst south of the dam would prove a fifty-foot channel too narrow. [21]

By then Mayor Tobin was back in town. Widening the channel would be "a useless waste of money," he said. There were only funds to finish a fifty-foot-wide channel, and that was wide enough. Besides, taxpayers would not stand for another bond issue, he added, promising, "We shall build it regardless of the protest filed." [22]

Undeterred, businessmen presented city commissioners with a petition containing forty-five signatures requesting a seventy-foot channel. Petitioners also sought early completion of the southern channel project to prevent "dumping floodwaters" on South Side residents—including those in the fine homes along King William Street, where so many families of German origin lived that the nearby curve in the river was known as Sauerkraut Bend. [23]

But then Mayor Tobin died, and Crecelius was on his own to justify the fifty-foot channel. Questioned, Crecelius claimed he couldn't recollect the width of the downtown river recommended by Metcalf & Eddy—it was seventy feet, not fifty—but in defense of fifty feet he cited numerous statistics, including

reduced costs. Commissioners went along with their engineer, and construction continued. Then everything came unglued. [24]

The new mayor, C. M. Chambers, challenged complaining businessmen to come up with "expert advice" to support their opinion. They produced Dallas engineer O. N. Floyd. Floyd determined that the narrower conduit could carry the estimated amount of water, given its slope and assuming that debris did not block its entrance. But he found a mistake in Crecelius's calculations. Corrected, they showed the velocity of water originally projected to enter the smaller channel as slower than it would be in reality. Floyd concluded that an uncovered seventy-foot channel would be required and that the cost would be less than Crecelius and the late Mayor Tobin had estimated. [25]

Crecelius admitted the error. Two days later the wider channel was approved. Amid reports that the mayor would fire him, Crecelius submitted his resignation. But businessmen persuaded the mayor not to hold Crecelius responsible "for the turn things had taken." Chambers, apparently believing that Crecelius's contract was legally binding for the duration of the project, did not accept the resignation but cut the flood engineer's salary by 40 percent. Six months later the mayor closed the flood prevention office and put the program under the city engineer. This time, Crecelius resigned for good. [26]

The mayor then reopened the flood prevention office and hired the Fort Worth firm of Hawley & Freese, in association with O. N. Floyd, to work things out. Hawley & Freese picked former city engineer Hans Helland as its resident engineer.[27] Work on the cutoff channel remained at a near standstill for a year, while right-of-way for the wider channel was acquired and another $500,000 in bonds was approved. During the lull, downtown businessmen saw their chance.[28]

The Great Bend's cutoff channel would be as wide as the Great Bend itself. Why should the expensive bypass sit empty when it could just as easily carry the regular flow of the Great Bend? Especially when, unless "scores" of artesian wells were drilled to augment the declining flow, "within ten years" the river would be dry anyway? Why not just fill in the Great Bend now?[29]

Reported one newspaper in mid-February 1928: "Prominent businessmen are said to be meeting in closed conferences, outlining a process by which they can press city commissioners to reclaim this portion of the river when the psychological time arrives— upon the completion of the 'Big Bend' cutoff." The unnamed businessmen had statistics. The Great Bend took up 294,000 square feet—nearly seven acres—of prime downtown real estate. The old riverbed could be sold for between $2 million and $14.7 million, and the city would get the funds. "At least three real estate promoters" went to work.[30]

The promoters, however, did not get far. "Numerous civic clubs" met to oppose the plan, which faced a "well-defined countermovement . . . particularly among women's clubs of the city." Fire and Police Commissioner Phil Wright said city officials had discussed the matter among themselves, and that "every one of them is unalterably opposed to any plan to reclaim the old river bed in the big bend."[31] Council members vied with each other for the strongest condemnation of the idea.

"As long as I am in this office the Big Bend channel will never be filled up," thundered Mayor Chambers. "I am absolutely against abandoning the river. In my opinion the San Antonio River is one of the biggest assets of this city." Tax Commissioner Frank Bushick said he "would never vote for it under any circumstances." Street Commissioner Paul Steffler believed that "to abandon the river would be a crime." He thought rerouting storm sewers emptying into the bend alone would cost almost as much as the value of the reclaimed land.[32]

The Great Bend would remain. But the businessmen had one last card to play.

One of the choicest undeveloped areas adjacent to downtown was along the southern bank of the Great Bend's southern leg—the rundown neighborhood of ancient structures in La Villita, settled in Spanish times. The noose had tightened around La Villita as surrounding streets were widened, improving access and opportunities. All that was missing was a direct north-south street into downtown. Filling the Great Bend would have made one easy. But even with the Great Bend still in place, such a street was not impossible. Developers quietly laid their plans.[33]

Businessmen in the eastern part of downtown were organized as the Eastside Improvement League, headed by John H. Kirkpatrick, the "conquering hero" who had arrived in the river parade as fiesta king twenty-one years before. At the close of 1928, city commissioners promised the Improvement League that they would spend $100,000 to extend Losoya Street southeast to meet South Alamo Street at Market Street. But when funding was approved three months later, Losoya Street was instead to extend southwest, crossing Market Street to reach Villita Street.

To get there, the new forty-five-foot-wide street would pass over a parallel section of the Great Bend. At some points the entire street would overhang the river, leaving only twenty-five feet of the river and its banks visible from above. The as yet unplanned Arneson River Theater would have been in the shadow of the bridge.[34]

Eighteen days after unanimously approving the project, city commissioners were swearing it would never happen. For when residents comprehended the impact of the overhang, it "met with a storm of protests from all sections of the city." Assistant City Engineer T. H. Coghill admitted that his staff drew up the new plans with help from the Eastside Improvement League. A few days later, however, city engineers said they had only just then realized that much of the street would have to be built over the river.[35]

Armed with that revelation, Mayor Chambers branded the attempt to take space above the river "grand larceny." He made it clear that his administration would "not tolerate any such plans." The mayor refused to let a four-member delegation from the Eastside Improvement League even present arguments, and termed a suggested tour of the site, to see where the street would cross City Water Board property, a waste of time.[36]

The businessmen felt betrayed. A meeting with Street Commissioner Paul Steffler was marked by "heated verbal tilts." Real estate broker Ernest Altgelt complained that he had already spent $11,000 for options "on trashy shacks and dives" to line up

In 1928 a group of businessmen sought to cantilever an extended Losoya Street over the river into La Villita. The proposal was soundly rejected.

property "under the impression that the city was ready to proceed."[37]

After the commotion died down, the $100,000 for the Losoya Street project was approved as first intended, to extend the street southeast to South Alamo Street.[38] The still isolated pocket of La Villita was left to molder for another ten years, until it was rescued in a pioneering historic preservation project.

The cutoff channel project finally got moving again in March 1929, and the city set about staking its river property line to protect against encroachments. The action was buttressed by a recent Texas Supreme Court rejection, on a technicality, of a developer's attempt to circumvent the city and buy an abandoned river bend south of town from the state itself.[39]

That victory took some of the edge off the city's embarrassment as workers began tearing fifteen feet off the back of the city's new Police and Health Department Building to widen the cutoff channel. The just-completed structure was on the site of the historic 1855 French Building, purchased by the city with flood control funds since the deep building extended well into the site of the proposed channel. The French Building's limestone blocks were used to line the river channel from Travis Street north to the new auditorium. As concrete laid for the narrower channel was broken up and the channel widened, one workman died in the cave-in of an excavation beneath Commerce Street.[40]

A swath of buildings was cleared through the heart of the city as the channel was dug. Utility lines once beneath streets were propped up until they could be attached to the undersides of bridges being stretched across the new cut. As residents actually saw the

San Antonio's Big Dig came in 1929–30, as an open channel was cut through the center of downtown so floodwaters could flow straight rather than having to deal with the Great Bend. Existing utility lines were propped up to maintain service.

result, new controversy erupted. Stark concrete walls plunging twenty-six feet down on either side of an empty channel did not provide the ambience many San Antonians thought appropriate for their city. After one protest on the channel's "ugliness," Mayor Chambers grumped that it was "one of the biggest eyesores of the city and should be filled up."[41]

Then bids came in to line the channel south of downtown with concrete, as recommended by Hawley & Freese despite the mayor's preference for an earthen channel. Chambers had become increasingly frustrated by the slow progress and by the stream of delegations at his door with complaints about the river project. Chambers had escrow checks returned to all four bidders, fired Hawley & Freese, and ordered the city engineer to build a wider channel of dirt. He said this would be more attractive than concrete and much less expensive. Declared the irascible and quotable mayor: "We are not going to line the gutters with gold."[42]

When reminded that not building a concrete channel and leaving the trees would require the channel to be dug deeper, Mayor Chambers retorted: "Dig to Hades! I had rather spend a half million dollars beautifying this river than a million dollars making it a concrete-lined sewer." The earthen channel was made deeper, to await more changes decades later.[43]

Chambers's reluctance to spend more on flood control was well-founded. Since 1924, three bond issues had provided a total of $3.9 million. But by the fall of 1929 only $150,000 was left, and two major sections were as yet unfinished—the channel below Pioneer Flour Mills south of downtown and the channel above Municipal Auditorium.[44]

Beyond the auditorium, the river stretched northward for nearly three miles to its headwaters. Metcalf & Eddy had wanted the entire channel straightened and widened, leaving only "substantial well-rooted trees not too close together." Samuel Crecelius, the city's flood engineer, had thought it should also be lined with concrete. Those recommendations were ultimately rejected by the city, which did see wisdom, however, in straightening three bends as advised. Of those, the first, below Josephine Street, was straightened without incident early in 1929. Straightening the second and largest of the three, between Eighth and Tenth streets as far west as Central Catholic High School, began quietly in the fall of 1928 with condemnation proceedings against recalcitrant property owners, though economic conditions would delay its completion for nearly thirty years.[45]

Growth of San Antonio, meanwhile, was continuing at full bore, not hurt at all by awareness of the decreased likelihood of flooding downtown. Population growth during the decade exceeded 40 percent, soaring from 161,000 to 230,000. By mid-1928 fifteen construction projects, at a cost of $10 million alone, were under way, a record expected to double within six months. As the skyline grew upward, it was also, inevitably, broadening. Neighborhoods once on downtown's fringe were being drawn into the core.[46]

One such spot was a natural, southeast of the intersection of Trenton Street—present-day McCullough Avenue—and North St. Mary's Street, a block north of the new auditorium. The twelve-acre site was about to be consolidated by a public project, elimination of the third bend in the river's northern channel. The Swiss Plaza Company proposed to loan the city $200,000 to straighten the bend and clear the trees so it could begin construction. Women's clubs, however, were standing by.[47]

The Woman's Club, the Conservation Society, and a Federation of Women's Clubs committee all filed formal protests with city hall. The federation pledged "united opposition" to any measure to further change the course of the river upstream or remove any vegetation at all, and went so far as to declare that the river was "being constantly menaced by the selfishness and greed of promoters and politicians."[48]

Then Swiss Plaza agreed to both donate the land and pay for the cutoff in exchange for the old riverbed. City commissioners accepted, after the federation dropped its opposition in return for the promise that the city would not pave the channel with concrete. The deal, however, went no further as hotel plans disintegrated with the worsening Depression, and the

One advocate for beautifying the San Antonio River was Gutzon Borglum, who was living in San Antonio while working on a monument to Texas trail drivers and preparing his initial designs for Mount Rushmore.

bend was not straightened until thirty years later—without a concrete channel.[49]

As the decade passed and elements of the flood control projects took final form, public attention was shifting from "Where should the river go?" back to "How should it look?" The first major river beautification drive since the 1921 flood came in 1928. Five thousand women were due in town for the national convention of the General Federation of Women's Clubs. The San Antonio Federation of Women's Clubs was determined to show its guests a tidy city and doled out assignments to the clubs making up its membership. The Old Spanish Trail Association got the task of overseeing river cleanup.[50]

Thanks to lobbying by the ladies of the Old Spanish Trail Association, the river park gained its first permanent river walk. Flagstones were laid to create a walkway along the west and south sides of the river, the same route businessmen twelve years earlier had targeted for a river walk. The walk extended for three blocks, south from Houston Street and around the start of the Great Bend to Navarro Street. Banks were sodded and flowers and shrubs planted, and a ligustrum hedge went in to screen unsightly backs of buildings.[51]

The federation assigned the task of overseeing ornamental lighting of the river to the Conservation Society, which persuaded the city to replace its strings of red, white, and blue lights with permanent flood-lights, artistically placed. Speaking for the society on the matter was a new honorary member—newly arrived sculptor Gutzon Borglum. Borglum set up a studio in the abandoned 1885 Water Works pump house in Brackenridge Park to work on a memorial to Texas trail drivers and to design his mock-ups for Mount Rushmore. He believed the river could be worth "millions" to the city and urged the purchase of gondolas and canoes for tourists.[52]

In 1930, as the cutoff channel was completed, no one seemed happy with how it looked. To soften its starkness, the city planted grass, flowers, and low shrubs on sod laid within the channel on either side of an open sixteen-foot median strip, which carried a small flow of water piped in to give the appearance of a natural stream. The city also had to reassure the Federation of Women's Clubs that water headed for the Great Bend would not be diverted into the new channel.[53]

There was still concern about the river going dry, but citizens showed more determination than in the previous decade. After a drought in the summer of 1927 threatened to dry up the river, there was no debate over putting a pump at a well near the headwaters to send water back in. The next summer an

underground sprinkler system was installed to keep the river's downtown banks green.[54]

A visiting official of the Southern States Art League urged local artists to paint along the river, assuring them it was "the most beautiful thing you have; it has anything New York has got beaten a thousand blocks."[55]

When completed, the downtown flood control cutoff channel gained landscaped banks at its base to soften the effects of the sheer concrete walls. The main flow was still around the Great Bend, shown emptying back into the main channel as the bend ended beside the Plaza Hotel at lower right.

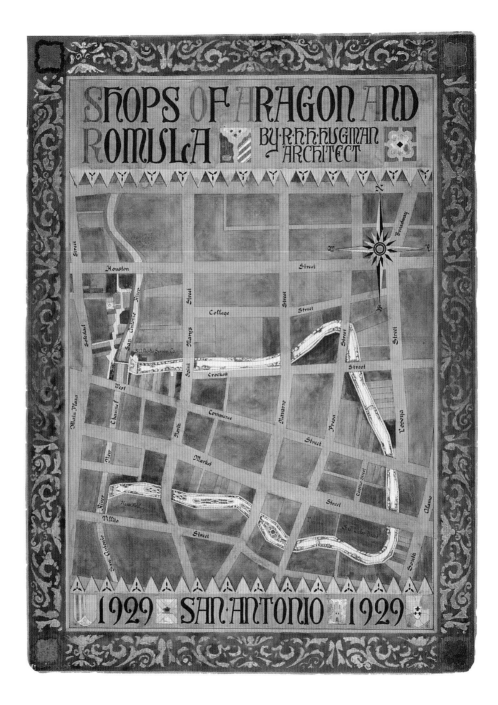

5
DEBATING THE RIVER PARK

A dam was built, the river was straightened, and the Great Bend not only kept its trees but gained gates to divert into an alternate channel whatever high waters headed its way. Catastrophic flooding was in the past.

Now what?

It would take ten years for that question to be resolved. The choices came down to opposing plans advanced by two men whose backgrounds could hardly have been more different.

Robert Harvey Harold Hugman, twenty-seven, had close-cropped dark hair rimming a high forehead, a sporty moustache that tapered past both ends of his upper lip, and was fond of holding a long, straight-stemmed pipe. He looked out from youthful dark eyes with the sensitive gaze of a dreamer. Born to a working class family on San Antonio's south side, he studied architecture at the University of Texas in Austin. After a

stint in New Orleans, he returned to San Antonio to open a practice in architecture, and needed more work. He saw the San Antonio River as a chance to exploit the city's Spanish heritage with a fanciful mix of shops and open space.[1]

Harland Bartholomew, forty, was clean-shaven, and combed his graying hair straight back. His aquiline nose supported a pair of round, thin steel-rimmed glasses that accented the steady, appraising look of a professional long accustomed to sizing up a situation and moving forward. Bartholomew was born in Stoneham, Massachusetts, spent his early years on a farm in New Hampshire, and studied engineering at Rutgers University in New Jersey. He was director of city planning for St. Louis, and the first full-time planner hired by an American city. On the side he ran his own consulting firm. During the first six years of the 1920s

opposite page
Robert Hugman's first plans for the River Walk showed an entrance through the Book Building on Houston Street down a new cobblestone lane past the shops of Aragon to river level and into the Great Bend, which he then termed Romula.

left
Robert Hugman, above, 27 and just starting out as an architect, had a romantic plan for the river, including river-level shops. Harland Bartholomew, 40, below, the nation's leading urban planner, favored keeping the river as a linear park, with any shops at the street level above.

Harland Bartholomew and Associates did twenty of the nation's eighty-seven comprehensive city plans, nearly twice as many as the closest competitor. He saw the San Antonio River as a rare ribbon of calm through a busy metropolis, its use best restricted to imaginative landscaping; any Spanish shops should be at street level along a pedestrian mall affording serene views of an enhanced river park below.[2]

Robert Hugman was the first out of his corner. When he walked into the office of San Antonio Mayor C. M. Chambers in May 1929, he was armed with little more than the enthusiasm of youth and a plan for the San Antonio River. He had been captivated by

the way New Orleans emphasized its French heritage in preserving the French Quarter, and was coming to ask the mayor why San Antonio shouldn't capitalize on its Spanish heritage by enlivening the narrow park along the river. Spanish Colonial Revival, after all, was already the dominant new architectural style in the city and throughout the Southwest. Similar motifs could, he believed, be adapted to the river's landscape. To accomplish this, Hugman had some bold ideas. He was eager to share them.

Robert Hugman's background contrasted sharply not only with those of leading national planners, but with those of leading San Antonio architects in the first decades of the twentieth century. Alfred Giles, James Riely Gordon, Harvey Page, George Willis all came from somewhere else, drawn by opportunities of designing some of the new construction in one of the nation's fastest-growing cities; Giles and Page had years earlier presented dramatic river improvement drawings that were applauded and then ignored. Many other top architects who did grow up in San Antonio—Ralph Cameron, Atlee B. Ayres, Robert M. Ayres—had sterling credentials from the Northeast and often from Europe, and frequently enjoyed close ties to the local business and social establishment.

Hugman benefited from few of those advantages, and was quite young to boot. One of his first major commissions was a residence at 230

Mexico City's water gardens of Xochimilco inspired Robert Hugman with their poled flat-bottom boats and waterside restaurants.

West King's Highway in 1929 for early river activist T. Noah Smith, though it does not quite measure up to the distinctiveness of neighboring homes. In urban landscape design, Hugman's perspective came not from the firsthand observations San Antonio's well-traveled architects could bring from the Old World, but from books.

"We read descriptions of the old cities of Spain," Hugman wrote, "of a narrow, winding street barred to vehicular traffic yet holding the best shops, clubs, banks and cafes; prosperous, yet alluring, with its shadowed doorways and quaint atmosphere. . . . It occurred to me that such a street in the very heart of our growing city would do much to enhance its interest and naught to impair its progress."[3]

An inspiration he cited closer to home was Xochimilco, Mexico City's colorful water gardens. Dating from the tenth century, they were shallow enough that boats could be poled along, as Hugman envisioned for San Antonio's river.[4] In his own hometown he could see some fanciful rockwork in San Pedro Park and more in the Japanese Sunken Gardens, the post–World War I municipal transformation of a rock quarry pit with curving waterside walks and narrow, arching pedestrian bridges built of the abundant native limestone. Hugman may also have been aware of the elaborate 1920s development of Coral Gables, Florida, the new Miami suburb where a former quarry had been converted into the Venetian Pool, Mediterranean architecture abounded along a

San Antonio already had romantic water-related limestone construction before the River Walk, including arched bridges in the Japanese Sunken Gardens, left, and at least one stairway in San Pedro Park, right.

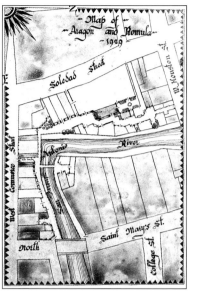

The 1929 map at right shows how Hugman first planned his shopping lane to descend from Houston Street to the river. At center left it would have crossed a low dam across the river to reach shops inside the Great Bend. The structure shown across the bend at that point is a floodgate, largely redesigned as Hugman first envisioned, far right.

new system of canals, and where the developer, Charles Merrick, dreamed of "castles in Spain made real."[5]

For San Antonio, Robert Hugman envisioned beginning a romantic street where river planners had focused for the previous sixteen years: near the centrally located Houston Street bridge, then the busiest span over the river. The entrance would be near the southwest corner of the bridge, apparently a new passage cut through the first floor of the three-story red brick Book Building. It would open at the rear to a "typical old Spanish patio" overlooking the river.[6]

Visitors would then descend along a narrow cobblestone street, the fanciful stone and brick shops of Aragon on either side. At the foot of the street the river would come into view again, near the start of the new cutoff channel, where the original channel turned 90 degrees into the Great Bend. There an outdoor cafe would be located.

From the cafe, a footbridge would arch the cutoff channel to the southern bank of the Great Bend and Romula past a floodgate screened by a stone Spanish-style gate with arched openings. A row of small shops was planned on the right bank and a small courtyard with larger shops on the left bank. After the bend turned sharply south, between Crockett and Commerce streets, would be a row of river-level restaurants offering "foods of all nations." On the opposite side would be a row of shops. After the bend turned sharply west, the channel was to divide into two streams flowing through "a sunken garden of loveliness to compare with the famous Gardens of the Alcazar or the Alhambra." Gondolas would ferry visitors along the river to the new twelve-story Plaza Hotel, built in the popular Spanish Colonial Revival style at the end of the bend.[7]

Before going to see the mayor, Robert Hugman called at the elegant West Magnolia Avenue home of Amanda Cartwright Taylor, who chaired the San Antonio Conservation Society's river committee. Armed with her encouragement, he went on to city hall. There he soon found himself a pawn in a larger game.[8]

Hugman's plan made a favorable impression on Mayor Chambers. In a "To Whom It May Concern" memo dated May 29, 1929, Chambers wrote:

I consider the Shops of Aragon and Romula to be a municipal improvement that will do much to preserve and enhance the distinctiveness of San Antonio, and as such it deserves the enthusiastic support of our loyal citizenship.

The City has not accepted the plan of Mr. Hugman, but heartily endorses same, and if Mr. Hugman receives proper cooperation from owners along [the] route, we feel reasonably sure that the City will adopt same and begin work without delay.[9]

Armed with that endorsement, a month later Hugman took his finished drawings to make a formal presentation to thirty business, civic, and political leaders, including the mayor and two commissioners.

Robert Hugman planned commercial activity for both sides of his River Walk between Crockett and Commerce streets. On the west bank, above, the existing Clifford Building at left and Casino Club at right would anchor a restaurant development entitled "Foods of All Nations." On the opposite bank, below, would be a series of riverside shops.

This favorite section of the river park between Navarro and St. Mary's streets, shown in the 1930s, included a landscaped cascade, right center, carrying air conditioning water runoff from the Majestic Theatre a block away. A few years later the cascade was redesigned as an integral part of the River Walk.

He stressed that his plan was of commercial value and must not be separated into parts. "Like a stage setting designed and directed by one mind to produce the proper unity of thought and feeling," it needed to be carried out as a unit, "shops, lighting effects, advertising—everything." Most of those present pledged support. Two days later, the text of Hugman's proposal was published in the *Light*.[10]

In scarcely two weeks, however, the plan was sidelined not by opponents of river beautification, but by proponents of a long-sought goal of progressive San Antonians—a comprehensive city plan.

Hiring a professional planner had been a prime objective of the civic reformers who captured control of city hall in 1912. But fund-raising to hire the noted George Kessler flagged after Mayor Augustus Jones's sudden death, leaving San Antonio without a master plan. Alert San Antonians had to look only as far as Dallas to see how such a plan—by Kessler, adopted there in 1912—was benefiting a metropolis on a growth curve rivalling San Antonio's. It was a point of pride to San Antonians that their city had always maintained a population lead of at least a few thousand over Dallas. As the 1920s headed to a close, the specter of Dallas's aggressive business establishment taking away San Antonio's crown as the largest city in Texas accelerated a Keep San Antonio First campaign. If San Antonians put their city's welfare ahead of their personal interests, the exhortations went, San Antonio could not help but remain first.[11]

This striving fit well with the renewed support for a plan to bring some sort of order to San Antonio's unchecked growth. This time the lead was taken by the Conservation Society and its cofounder, Rena Maverick (Mrs. Robert B.) Green. The ladies lobbied tirelessly for the cause. At the end of 1928 Mayor

Chambers began appointing fifty-six San Antonians to an advisory City Plan Committee.[12]

Within six months the committee recommended hiring Harland Bartholomew and Associates of St. Louis. The firm's work would cost $40,000. Chambers, in the midst of an economy drive, thought that was far too much. With a decision imminent, the mayor made a counterproposal: use Hugman's plan for the river and get a master plan for the rest of the city through a nationwide competition. Prizes would total $7,000, a significant savings from Bartholomew's fee.[13]

Leaders of the City Plan Committee, their hard-sought goal threatened at the last minute, would have none of it. Hugman's plan was blasted as no more than an "idle dream" by City Plan Committee Chairman Newton H. White, who also headed the Chamber of Commerce. His committee had already studied the river, White told the mayor and commissioners, and to

adopt Hugman's plan would set his group's work back six months. In any event, White added, Bartholomew himself recognized the need to preserve San Antonio's individuality and the river. Local city plan competitions had already failed to produce results. How could entrants from out of town do any better?[14]

Commissioners, after hearing three more forceful opponents of the mayor's suggestion, postponed a decision for three days. Then White and three of his committee members returned to plead the case for Bartholomew. Two speakers in the audience suggested that local architects and engineers be hired to do the master plan, and mentioned two candidates. The two were present, but rose and objected to doing the work. Harland Bartholomew was hired.[15]

Robert Hugman was assigned to political limbo, his backers in the Conservation Society preferring instead to support a city planner of Bartholomew's stature. That fall, the City Federation of Women's

At right, the double-towered apartment building that became the Havana Riverwalk Inn shows in this 1932 view of the river park. Municipal Auditorium's towers are visible at right of center. The view at left looks south past a sandbar caused by bank erosion to the Augusta Street bridge. The old Ursuline Academy is off the photo at right.

Clubs passed a resolution pleading that Hugman at least be hired as the river's landscape architect. The mayor replied that the question of Hugman's employment would have to wait.[16]

Bartholomew, whose firm emphasized working closely with municipal governments to build consensus, took an active personal role in the San Antonio project. He gave particular attention to river improvements, a subject that dominated his first official visit late in 1929. In three years his firm produced a 400-page comprehensive city plan, covering streets, transportation, transit, zoning, recreation, and civic art. The last category included a section titled "Proposed Treatment of the San Antonio River in the Central Business District."[17]

Bartholomew agreed that the San Antonio River was "one of the most distinctive and commendable features in the character of San Antonio. . . . To the visitor this is a picture not easily forgotten." He recommended a parkway along the river from downtown north through Brackenridge Park, an idea proposed the year before by Parks Commissioner Ray Lambert, to help make up for the city's deficiency in parkways and boulevards.[18] But the most detailed river analysis was reserved for the downtown section.

Bartholomew's approach to commerce was the reverse of Hugman's. Instead of adding shops and restaurants beside the river, the master planner recommended that commercial activity be kept at street level and that riverside landscaping below maintain a

natural, contemplative linear park through the heart of the busy city. Groupings of water elm, sycamore, cypress, and pecan trees were to provide shade, screen backs of buildings, and overhang the water. Low flowers and reeds would line the channel. Flowering native shrubs would break up the straight vertical lines of retaining walls and produce masses of color, and vines would climb walls and lattices and provide ground cover. Beside bridges, tall evergreen cypresses would frame river views, with date and banana palms adding a tropical note. There would be only a few benches. General recreation was ruled out as too distracting.

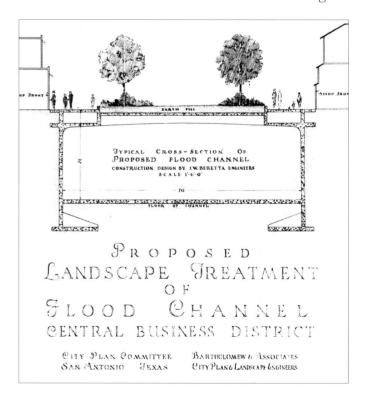

Planner Harland Bartholomew recommended covering the unsightly cutoff channel and turning it into a street with colorful shops on either side.

Bartholomew did find room in his plan for the sort of romantic shops Hugman had proposed for his Aragon and Romula. Engineers had told Bartholomew that the "ugly and glaring" cutoff channel could handle major floodwaters even if it were covered with a top of reinforced concrete. Bartholomew proposed turning such a cover into a pedestrian mall.

The new mall would have walkways ten feet wide on either side of a fifty-foot-wide grassy median, landscaped with cacti and native plants able to thrive on just two feet of earth fill. At each end a fountain and overlook would offer vistas of the main river channel.

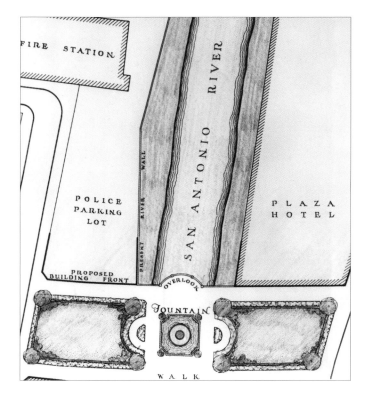

Buildings facing or backing on the new mall could have doorways cut through to create shop facades with the sort of aging ambiance that later emerged as doorways were cut into existing basement walls along the River Walk. Additional colorful shops would be built on vacant lots, providing an overall total of 950 feet of new retail frontage that would generate tax revenues to pay for the project.[19]

Though Bartholomew's solution may neatly have addressed beautification of both the river and the yawning cutoff channel, by the time the plan was finished and formally recommended to city commissioners it was March 1933. The full force of the Depression had plunged downtown San Antonio into a slump from which it would not recover for nearly forty years. San Antonio's building boom was at an abrupt end, city hall lost nearly 20 percent of a full year's operating funds in the city's worst bank failure, and there were massive layoffs of municipal workers. It didn't help that, despite all of San Antonio's strivings, by 1930 Dallas had overcome San Antonio's population lead to become the largest city in Texas.

Then, in the month Bartholomew's plan was presented to the city, C. M. Chambers became San Antonio's fourth mayor in twenty-one years to die while in office. Some recommendations, including the city's first zoning and a street plan, had been implemented along the way, but other major recommendations would obviously go on hold.[20]

Harland Bartholomew's plan for San Antonio was to preserve the river park as a ribbon of serenity in a busy city. It could be enjoyed from overlooks, such as from this portion of a covered cutoff channel.

In April 1936 ceremonies on the river park's embankment below Crockett Street, Mollie Bond Hayes, representing the Alamo Chapter of the Daughters of the American Revolution, christens one of two motorboats beginning service to the Houston Street bridge.

Despite the lack of action on either Hugman's or Bartholomew's plans, the city did not abandon river beautification. Renewed efforts focused on the old Tobin Terrace, the banks below Crockett Street between the St. Mary's and Navarro street bridges. In 1934, City Parks Commissioner Jacob Rubiola's Parks Department restored the riverside cascade built ten years earlier on the riverbank behind St. Mary's College. The next spring, parks workers wrapped ten new flowerbeds nearby in low walls of native stone.[21]

By this time, San Antonio's vaunted self-reliance of the previous decade was but a memory. Not only were federal funds now subsidizing unemployed former city workers to inaugurate or improve municipal projects, they were also helping such professionals as young architects who ventured out on their own just before the economy crashed. Robert Hugman, for one, had found employment as a consulting landscape architect for the federal government's Works Progress Administration in San Antonio. In 1935 he supervised WPA design of a section along Walnut Creek in Seguin's Starke Park, thirty miles east of San Antonio, with walkways and stone elements presaging those of San Antonio's River Walk. Still, Hugman could not forget his shops of Aragon and Romula. He continued to promote those plans to all who would listen, hoping for some way to revive them.[22]

The spark came, unexpectedly, from the Texas Centennial in 1936.

One group that heard Hugman was the Alamo Chapter of the Daughters of the American Revolution. The DAR made "beautifying and conserving the natural charm of the San Antonio River" a chapter centennial project. Unable to get city funds to light the Great Bend between Travis and Nueva streets at night, the Daughters got the money instead from the city's privately organized Centennial Committee, which relied on state and federal funding. The river was soon drawn into the upcoming events.[23]

San Antonio's major centennial celebration began at the Alamo at sunup on March 5, 1936—one hundred years after the siege—and continued throughout the day, including speeches, concerts, parades, presentations, a Pontifical High Mass, and a flyover by nine bombers from Kelly Field. The ascendant city of Dallas may have out-hustled San Antonio to land the Texas Centennial Exposition, complete with a reproduction of the Alamo, but the message was clear that San Antonio still had the real Alamo. And, unlike Dallas, San Antonio had a river to celebrate on as well.[24]

In April came Fiesta, made even more elaborate that anniversary year with the first "Venetian" carnival and river parade in twenty-nine years, now that events could be scheduled on the Great Bend without fear of washout by sudden storms. Also, San Antonio's flood prevention program had passed its first big test the previous summer, when twenty feet of water built up by heavy rains were held behind Olmos Dam. As floodgates dropped and shielded the bend, floodwaters, reduced by the dam, flowed without incident through the cutoff channel.[25]

At the opening of Fiesta week, on the banks of the old Tobin Terrace the DAR ceremoniously christened two flower-bedecked motorboats, complete with canvas awnings with scalloped fringes, to begin commercial trips from the Houston Street bridge. The next day, April 21, more than 10,000 people crowded riverbanks near the Plaza Hotel to watch a parade of eighteen decorated boats. Two bands played, a company of dancers performed, and flower girls in Mexican costumes strolled the banks. Gondola rides began the next day at a landing near the Plaza. Observing all this was A. C. (Jack) White, thirty-nine, the astute manager of the Plaza Hotel and co-chairman of events. White sensed far

During Fiesta in April 1936, a Texas Centennial river parade past the Plaza Hotel, at left edge of photo, helped revive general interest in activities along the downtown San Antonio River.

A snapshot of diners at the Rocking M Dude Ranch was enclosed in a folder advertising the bistro's location on Riverside Walk, overlooking the river park between Houston and Travis streets.

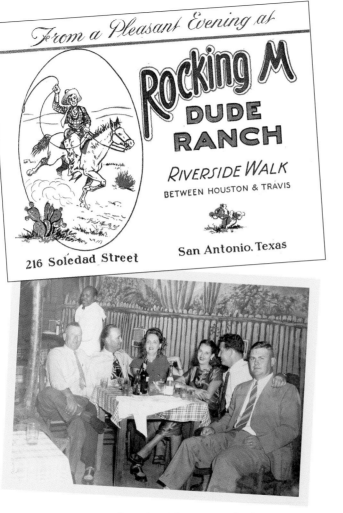

more opportunity for the Plaza—and the city—in Hugman's commercial River Walk orientation.[26]

Indeed, the Houston Street bridge destination of the new boats had become a growing focus of what then passed in San Antonio for river-oriented commerce. Houston Street's Riverside Restaurant, with its balcony jutting over the river park, still prospered at the bridge's southeast corner. Across the street, a blocklong sidewalk named Riverside Walk now extended along the upper edge of the eastern retaining wall overlooking the river from Houston Street up to Travis Street. One business facing Riverside Walk was the appropriately named Rio Vista Mexican Restaurant. Another was a bistro named the Rocking M Dude Ranch.

The new boats coming from the Plaza Hotel could tie up at Adolph Obadal's Riverside Gardens in the basement of the Book Building at the foot of the Houston Street bridge, where The Coffee House and the shorter-lived Riverside Club were open in the 1920s. Obadal counted on Olmos Dam to keep his restaurant dry. Alas, heavy rains on June 30, 1936, built up so much water behind the dam that its gates were opened to reduce the level. Water surging through the downstream channel rose nearly to the ceiling of Riverside Gardens. Adolph Obadal, listed in local directories prior to his restaurant venture as a "showman," forsook the river and moved on to the Sunset Novelty Company.[27]

The stirrings of riverside businesses near the Houston Street bridge pointed to commercial potential along the river. But to be successful, the lesson of Riverside Gardens showed, these businesses would best be within the floodgate-protected Great Bend. The lesson of the Centennial river parade was that such business did not have to depend on existing crowds on Houston Street; crowds would be drawn to the bend by specific events and most probably by Hugman's semicommercial environment.

The Depression and a changing guard at city hall had sapped the momentum of planner Harland Bartholomew's concept for a pastoral river park. Its advocates would rally for a limited rearguard victory over the competing plan, but the river's future belonged to the vision of Robert Hugman.

RIVERSIDE GARDENS

HOUSTON STREET AT THE BRIDGE

DRINKS
BILL of FARE

PLEASE PAY WHEN SERVED

During a convention of Spanish-American War veterans in 1935, the Riverside Gardens along the river park sought to draw customers by promoting itself as the "Official San Juan Canteen."

6
CREATING THE RIVER WALK

Jack White, fresh from the success of the 1936 extravaganza on the river, was well-tested in the ways of making up his mind and getting things done. Born on a cotton farm near Weatherford and orphaned when he was six, he worked his way through grade school and high school. At the age of sixteen he came to San Antonio as assistant manager of the Gunter Hotel. Ten years later he was made manager of the new Robert E. Lee Hotel. After two years, in 1925, he left to manage the new Hilton Hotel in Dallas. Two years later he was back in San Antonio as opening manager of the twelve-story Plaza Hotel.[1]

It was White's job to challenge the doyen of San Antonio hostelries, the St. Anthony, five blocks to the northeast. Soon rising across the street from the Plaza was the tallest building in Texas, the thirty-one story, six-

sided landmark first called the Smith-Young Tower. Sears & Roebuck occupied the ground floor. This was not the serene setting of the St. Anthony, which faced Travis Park.

The Plaza—and its restaurant—did, however, overlook the San Antonio River, a little bedraggled at that point, but with potential of its own. After all, the 1936 river parade had drawn more than 10,000 people practically to the Plaza's doors. White could see that he had a competitive edge worth exploiting, one that could be sold on the basis of its appeal to San Antonio alone. It was a task suited to his prodigious energy.

White laid his groundwork carefully and quietly. In January 1938 a committee of riverside property owners under White's chairmanship formed as the nucleus of the San Antonio

opposite page
As the Arneson River theater took shape in mid-1939, its concrete bleachers were made to look as if they were made of rock cut into the riverbank.

left
A new landmark at the end of the Great Bend was the Plaza Hotel, later Granada Homes, shown in 1928 as construction was beginning, lower left, on the 31-story Smith-Young Tower, later known as the Tower Life Building.

River Beautification Association. Members contributed enough to hire architect Robert Hugman and engineer Edwin P. Arneson for surveys and drawings based on Hugman's original proposals. San Antonio's Henry P. Drought, state administrator for the federal Works Progress Administration, the anticipated source of the major funding, was kept posted from the beginning.[2]

Plans were revealed to the public on the last Sunday in April, immediately following Fiesta week, when San Antonians, no longer distracted by Fiesta activities, could view the drawings on display in the Plaza Hotel. A formal request for partial city funding for the river project went before city council four days later.[3]

When the proposal was announced, there was none of Hugman's previous "sunken garden of loveliness" verbiage, and the terms "Aragon" and "Romula" had disappeared. With promotional tips from advertising executive Tom McNamara, White declared that this project would make San Antonio nothing less than the Venice of America.[4]

Said White, careful not to speak just for himself: "The committee believes that the river can be made the outstanding beauty spot of this country. Other cities can have beautiful parks, great zoos, magnificent stadiums, and other attractions, but we know of no city that has a beauty spot such as we propose to make of the river. . . . It would attract unlimited publicity to the city from newspapers, magazines, newsreels, and other mediums. A boat ride on the San Antonio River would attract tourists to this city as the gondolas do to Venice."[5]

The full length of the old river park would be transformed, plus a few blocks more to the north past Municipal Auditorium to the Fourth Street/ Lexington Avenue bridge. The idea of a major entrance through a row of shops descending down a cobblestone street from Houston Street to the river was abandoned in favor of broader access down more than two dozen new stairways from adjoining streets. Walls lining the northern river park's main channel would be replaced, and low rock features would be added. More extensive construction in the northern section, nearly a mile long, would interfere with flood control. Thus the new River Walk's major features would be in the flood-protected three-quarter-mile arc of the Great Bend, then usually referred to as the Horseshoe Bend or the Big Bend.

Hugman's most dramatic new drawing, with engineering input from Edwin Arneson, featured an outdoor theater with seats on one side of the river and a stage on the other. Between acts, a spray from the river in between would create a curtain of water. Other drawings showed decorative gate structures at each end of the bend. Along walkways beside the bend's terraced banks, new doors cut into the backs of existing buildings would become "beautiful front entrances of shops, cafes, etc., so that visitors and residents of the city could shop from a gondola."[6]

Cost estimates for the project started out at $265,000. If the city would appropriate $50,000, the businessmen would assess property owners along the river from Municipal Auditorium to the Plaza Hotel $2.50 per foot and raise another $40,000. Once that $90,000 was raised locally, the Works Progress Administration would contribute the remaining two-thirds. But city commissioners, under pressure to reduce expenses, declined to bring the matter to a public vote to raise funds through a bond issue. At least one commissioner, Frank Bushick, didn't get the big picture. Declaring his opposition to anything that would increase the city's tax burden, Bushick said: "This is a special issue which will benefit only a few people, the property owners along the river. The property owners are not small homeowners, but are big businessmen."[7]

City funding was only "delayed," hoped White, as a month later he announced that the $30,000 pledged so far by river property owners "has exceeded even our fondest expectations." Still far short of the additional $60,000 he needed, he made a pass at replacing the city funding with state funding through the Texas State Parks Board.[8]

After that ploy proved fruitless, White had a breakthrough. A once common technique to raise improvement funds for a limited area—unused in San Antonio since 1919—was for its residents to petition to form an improvement district. The residents would then vote on whether to tax themselves to raise their own bond funds.[9]

White outlined an area approximately a block and a half on each side of the river between Municipal Auditorium and the Plaza Hotel. He got ninety property owners within that area to petition the city for permission to form an improvement district. The goal was to raise $75,000 in bonds, covering the $60,000 once hoped for from the city plus another $15,000 apparently not yet contributed by property owners.[10]

City commissioners promptly authorized the district. Within this slice of downtown were as many as 1,300 property owners, though only 107 lived within it and were eligible to vote. Those few, however, owned $20 million—two-thirds—of its $32 million in assessed property value. A vote was set for October 25. On election day, 76 of the 107

River Beautification Board Chairman Jack White broke ground for the WPA River Walk project at Navarro Street's Mill Bridge on March 29, 1939.

residents cast ballots. The bond proposal passed 74 to 2.[11]

In the wake of the vote, Mayor C. K. Quin and the council named an eight-member San Antonio River Central Improvement Committee, later referred to as the River Beautification Board, to coordinate work with the city.[12] WPA funds were expedited through the efforts of San Antonio Congressman Maury Maverick, an ally of President Franklin D. Roosevelt. Roosevelt is said to have instructed Secretary of the Interior Harold Ickes, in his characteristic accent: "Harold, give Maury the money for his damn rivah so he will stop bothering me."[13]

As architectural and engineering plans were finalized, the project began to draw national attention, as Jack White had predicted. A February *New York Times* travel story was headlined, "Gondolas For Texans: San Antonio to Convert City Stream Into an 'American Venice.'" The *Times* reported the development would give "San Antonio a main street such as no other city will have and [make] it 'the city where you shop from gondolas.'"[14]

On the morning of March 29, 1939, San Antonio's WPA-funded Tipica Orchestra played Mexican favorites as 300 San Antonians gathered at Navarro Street's Mill Bridge to watch Jack White wield a golden shovel

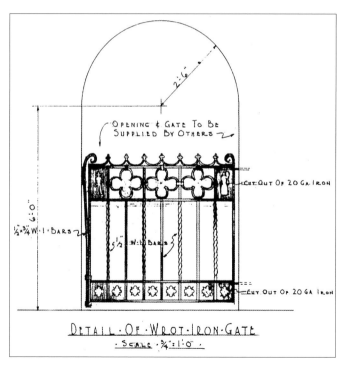

Decorative iron gates were designed for street-level entries to River Walk stairways but never installed. At far right, River Walk architect Robert Hugman checks details of the new rustic cedar and stone stairway, later replaced with concrete stairs, at the northwest corner of the Crockett Street bridge.

and break ground for the River Walk. Construction began quickly, despite a change in engineers. Edwin Arneson, fifty, the engineer who worked on the preliminary drawings, had died three months earlier after a brief illness. Arneson was replaced by Walter H. Lilly, who also got the task of preparing WPA grant applications for various segments of the project.[15]

Hugman seemed to gain even more enthusiasm as his long-anticipated work finally got started. During an interview with the *Express*, Hugman held his straight-stemmed pipe and spoke "rapidly for a native-born Texan" as he outlined, in paraphrasing by the reporter, his "colorful street in Mexico transplanted to downtown San Antonio. Here a potter will spin his wheel, shaping the simple pieces to delight visitors. A basket weaver may be next door. A few paces away, a Latin-American florist will be tempting a visitor with exotic blooms. All the business that flourishes below the Rio Grande, lazily and charmingly conducted, will be found here." Adding to the ambience would be swans and water pheasants, floating islands, adobe shops, and brightly colored tile work.[16]

Finalizing the break with the modern city above would be cedar cut for rustic benches, light posts, and steps on at least one bridge, plus signage in wrought iron letters. At Crockett Street, hand-hewn railings and steps of cedar logs would add a rustic note but provide a slippery footing; they were later replaced with more dependable stone steps and metal railings.

His drawings show there were to be four types of stone steps: those of informal stone, stone treads on concrete risers, cast stone on concrete risers and gravel steps for ascending terraces. Decorative iron gates at street level would lend a dramatic sense of entrance to the secluded world below.[17]

Understated design was paramount. Said Hugman: "I'll die if it looks like Hollywood."[18]

As the project unfolded, Hugman predicted that within two years businessmen would spend as much as $5 million of their own money on retail development along the river. He noted, though, "The bonds and the WPA can only create the opportunity. That's

A Hugman-designed column of twisted bricks supports the stairway descending from the southeast corner of the Crockett Street bridge, left. At right, a rustic cedar lightpost and railing below the South St. Mary's Street bridge are among original River Walk features that have not survived.

as far as public agencies can go in developing the river street."[19]

But before people could shop from gondolas, a basic engineering problem had to be addressed. The Great Bend descended about seven feet from beginning to end, a downward drop that could speed boats downstream but that caused a current a bit too swift for gondoliers poling upstream.

The solution was to decrease the drop from seven feet to one foot and thus slow the current by building

A Spanish-style gateway hiding floodgates at the northern entrance of the Great Bend was completed as designed by Robert Hugman.

an elaborate structure beside the Plaza Hotel at the end of the bend. This was designed with a double dam that would also work for flood control. The upper dam would be semicircular, curving in a gentle arc of forty feet so water would form a smooth curtain as it flowed into an oval pool four feet below. From there the water would spill over a straight-edged second dam into the cutoff channel, then flow on downstream. A footbridge arching the lower dam would become part of the St. Mary's Street sidewalk above.[20]

As for the bend's channel, shallow places had to be dug out and deep ones filled to gain a consistent depth of approximately three and a half feet, deep enough for gondoliers' poles and also shallow enough to guard against drowning for anyone falling from a gondola or from sidewalks close to the river's edge. Dredging—much of it with shovels and wheelbarrows—removed from the riverbed thousands of truckloads of refuse, ranging from broken wagon wheels and wrecked bicycles to tangled barbed wire and sunken barrels that once served as floats for bathhouses. When workers dredging the river's sharp turn below Augusta Street came up with thousands of crawfish in the mud, they dubbed the curve Crawfish Bend.[21]

Then there were the channel's existing concrete-covered stone walls, completed under George Surkey, the city's river commissioner, in 1914. Hugman thought these extended too starkly above the water line and also "confined the water to an extremely

Raising the water level of the Great Bend in an aesthetically pleasing manner to make the flow gentler was a challenge solved by a double dam in a carefully landscaped area ending with an archway supporting a street-level sidewalk.

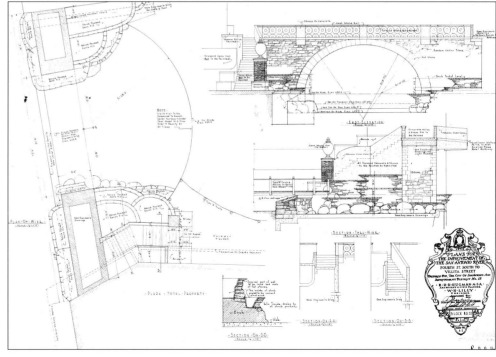

unnatural bank line." He proposed that new walls—of native limestone and not covered by concrete—bend gently and unevenly, almost imperceptibly in some places, to give the impression that they followed natural contours.[22]

Beside the banks Hugman preferred "simple gravel walks," though these were overruled by engineers as impractical. Instead there would be walks of flagstones, cobblestone, brick, concrete blocks, and cement inlaid with pebbles. They would feature nearly a dozen geometric designs, some with colored effects, to maintain a sense of ongoing discovery. Hugman had the panels' walkability tested by women wearing shoes with different types of heels.

Walkways periodically bowed out to become boat landings edged with vertical cedar posts to which gondolas could tie up.[23]

Where supports for the North Presa Street bridge created a sharp corner drop with no space for a path, Hugman designed a walkway—with a railing—that swung widely around the corner on supports leaving it barely above the water, making the walk appear to float. Added drama would come from the glow of electric lights beneath the walk.[24]

At several points, large drainpipes several feet above the level of the river emerged from retaining walls, some disgorging runoff from air-conditioning systems of major buildings, while others were storm

A series of geometric designs were embedded in sidewalk slabs to give strollers an ongoing sense of anticipation and surprise. At far right, the complication of a 90-degree turn in the river beneath the North Presa Street bridge was resolved with a low concrete sidewalk arcing around the sharp corner.

drains from streets above. These were disguised as springs.

On the north bank of the Great Bend, water from the Majestic Theatre's air conditioning system was already piped through a decorative cascade below the buildings of St. Mary's University, later the hotel Omni La Mansion del Rio, to flow down a concrete sluiceway into the river. Hugman rebuilt the cascade, flanked it with banana trees and decorative shrubs and allowed its water to flow into a pond and on into the river between flagstones integrated into the River Walk, which arced around the cascade.[25]

Downstream, under the Commerce Street bridge, a wide drainpipe pouring out runoff from Joske's Department Store's air conditioning was arched with honeycombed rock flanked with ferns, and designed to flow out beneath the narrow sidewalk. There was more room to work with on the upper River Walk's west bank north of Travis Street, where the Milam Building's air-conditioning system drained. At the base of the runoff pipe, water plants adorned a new pond with boulders added to slow the water's force. The pond's water, in turn, flowed into the river beneath a fanciful rock bridge amid lush plantings. Across the river, runoff from another outlet was to appear to be emerging from a newly built small cave.[26]

North of Travis Street, a stone bridge over an air conditioning runoff drain from the Milam Building made the water appear as a natural stream flowing into the river. Boulders around the outlet slowed the runoff's flow into the river.

A lighting system, controlled by eight switches hidden at intervals along the banks, would include floodlights, four types of wrought iron lanterns, colored lights at strategic points, and hidden bulbs below thick groupings of water plants. There were several gas streetlights. Descriptive plaques of colorful tiles made under the direction of Ethel Harris in another WPA project were set in retaining walls, one at the upper end of the bend to mark where a sniper in a tree picked off Texans in 1835 and the other beside the Mill Bridge and its historic ford.[27]

To link opposite shores, two narrow footbridges of limestone blocks, one on the northern leg and one on the southern, arched high enough so gondoliers could remain standing as they passed beneath. They became signature features of the River Walk. The west

This design of 154 tiles below the Mill Bridge and a smaller one at the northern gate to the Great Bend were made by artists employed in a separate WPA project.

OLD MILL CROSSING-LAST KNOWN PLACE WHERE HORSES DRANK AND FORDED THE RIVER.
DEDICATED TO THE MEMORY OF OUR FATHERS
ERECTED BY THE DAUGHTERS OF TEXAS TRAIL DRIVERS

bank of the upper River Walk would connect with the southern bank of the Great Bend by a walkway of stepping stones over the low dam that was diverting the right amount of water into the bend. The overflow slipping between the stepping-stones would create rapids as it passed over rocks on its descent into the cutoff channel.

Near the end of the bend, in the wide area that had once been a millpond, Hugman planned three floating islands—two small wooden rafts chained to either side of a larger raft, all anchored to large concrete blocks on the bottom by heavy chains fifteen feet long, allowing them to move with the current as well as to rise with high water. Hugman designed small huts to be built on the "islands" to house waterfowl.

The single most inspired feature of the River Walk, however, remains the open-air theater on the southern leg of the bend, its seats on one side and stage on the other, with boats able to pass between even during performances.

The river's naturally inward-curving, sharply rising south bank, across from the city's water pumping station, had become a dumping ground for several tons of auto and machine parts, which had to be cleared away. Concrete poured for curving tiers of bleachers, seating 1,000, was pounded to make them appear carved from natural rock. Sod was laid over the tops of the seats to lend a natural appearance. Above the top row rose the white stucco concession house and what was intended to be a movie projection room. Beside them an arched gateway led to the National Youth Administration's adjoining La Villita restoration, a favorite project of Maury Maverick, the former congressman and newly elected mayor.[28]

Across the narrow river from the inward-curving seating went the outward-curving stage, with tile-roofed dressing rooms and a backdrop of three narrow stone arches for hanging bells. A narrow bridge arched from stage right across to the seating area.

The complex was to be called the Broadcast Theater, where radio performances of miracle plays

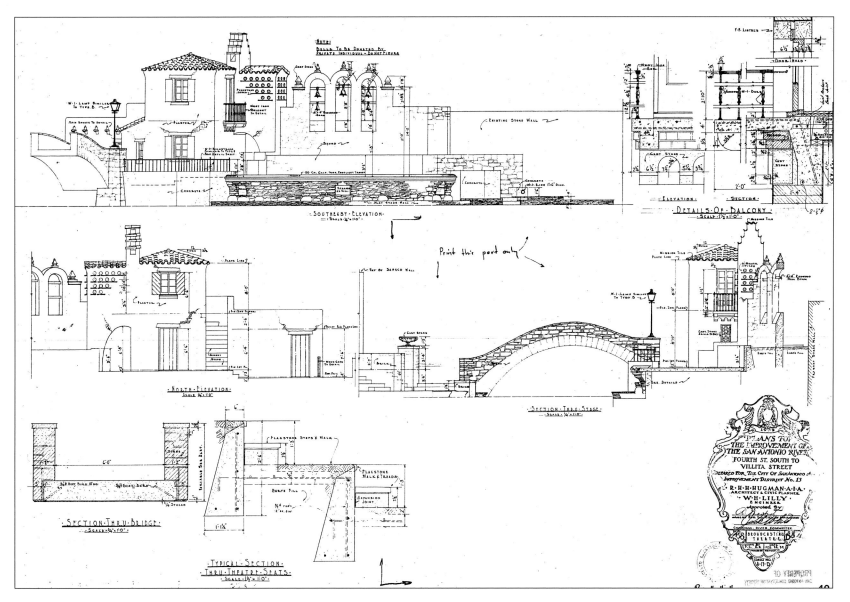

Robert Hugman's design for the river theater stage house
included tile-roofed dressing rooms, iron balconies, a
dovecote, an adjoining bridge, and a backdrop for bells.

of the Spanish Southwest and "other native drama" could originate. This function never materialized, and the theater was named instead in memory of Edwin Arneson, the engineer who worked on its preliminary planning.[29]

River Walk construction began with of a temporary coffer dam at the beginning of the Great Bend, diverting the river into the cutoff channel and leaving the bend with only puddles and a muddy trickle from nearby springs and runoff from above. Smoothing the river bottom could begin, new channel walls could be built and sidewalks laid, sometimes along one bank, sometimes along both. To clear the site for workmen,

existing plants and shrubs were transplanted to a temporary nursery off site. Remaining trees were kept watered and their roots protected. Decayed limbs were pruned, hollow trunks plugged with concrete, and weak trees braced.[30]

The work started with great enthusiasm. Hugman noticed that as he and Robert Turk, the project engineer, discussed things on site, "all the workmen within earshot would stop and listen intently to our conversation. We then purposely talked loud enough for them to hear and understand. They would then return to their work with added vigor and purpose."[31]

Turk praised the skill of the stonemasons. "They seemed to have a knack of knowing which rock to put where," he said. "When we would give a rock to a brick layer, he would chip around on it and get nowhere. But the stone masons got the job done."[32]

Two days before Christmas 1939, the coffer dam blocking the entrance of the Great Bend was removed. Jack White ceremoniously turned the valve to close the cutoff channel gate, sending water back into the bend for the first time since March. Another two months remained for planting—or transplanting from the temporary site—11,734 trees and shrubs, 1,500 banana trees, and 1,489 square

Sod covering of Arneson River Theater seats preserves the natural sense of being beside a river.

yards of grass. The project's final phase, lining the channel and landscaping from the start of the bend north to Municipal Auditorium, would start in the new year.[33]

But among those watching the project unfold, all was not well. The specter of the beloved river bend stripped of its plantings and of the bend's muddy channel churned up for walls, walks, stairways, and bridges in fanciful patterns of jarring, freshly cut limestone became too much for many San Antonians to bear, especially those who preferred the pastoral park recommended by the distinguished Harland Bartholomew. What did this Robert Hugman think he was doing?

Only three months into the project Hugman was having to defend himself. His design would soon be in "as naturalistic [a] setting as possible," he explained. "Everything is being done to avoid a raw, new, garish effect." The situation didn't bother Ernie Pyle, who filed a syndicated newspaper column from San Antonio praising the project while noting, "Right now the new bare stonework seems harsh and cold. But age and shrubbery will soften that."[34]

Locally, however, Hugman was finding critics in practically every direction. His former teacher at Brackenridge High School, Emily Edwards, cofounder of the San Antonio Conservation Society, did not like it, and asked to meet with her former student. A group

During construction of the River Walk, the Great Bend was drained and existing plantings were temporarily transplanted to nurseries for safety. At left, WPA workers prepare forms for the concrete stairway to the northwest corner of Navarro Street's Mill bridge.

of artists including the Conservation Society's other cofounder, Rena Maverick Green, a member of the City Plan Committee that endorsed Bartholomew's plan, resolved "that the stone work is much overdone, and looks so fantastic." Worse, Mrs. Green began complaining to her cousin Maury Maverick, the mayor. Even more ominously, Ruth White, the wife of Jack White, who oversaw Hugman's work, didn't like the way things were looking either.[35]

As work began in the upper channel past Houston Street to Municipal Auditorium, it was obvious that Hugman's pleas for patience—everything would mellow and look better with time—were not

Such unfamiliar shapes as that of this uncompleted pedestrian bridge plus the unkempt appearance of the drained riverbed disconcerted many San Antonians, leading to the discharge of River Walk architect Robert Hugman.

working. In January 1940 the increasingly influential Conservation Society passed a resolution condemning the project's "desecration of the beauties of San Antonio." The society also endorsed Rena Green's letter to the *Light*, entitled "A plea for simplicity in further landscaping of the river." The letter observed, "San Antonio is surrounded by rock quarries and our last two park commissioners were stone masons, so the temptation to excessive stone work was great." At the urging of Ruth White, a critique on the "excessive stone work" was sent to Hugman.[36]

Rena Green sent one copy of the Conservation Society's resolution to the eminent architect Atlee B. Ayres, who as chairman of a committee more than a quarter century earlier had backed a more conservative river project. Ayres replied that Hugman's work "was not done in a simple manner." He declared flatly: "With few exceptions, it is a most unwise expenditure and will be a source of ridicule to our tourist friends and others. I do hope that we won't have any more of this misnamed river beautification."[37]

Mrs. Green sent another copy of the resolution to Hugman, who could only respond with his familiar refrain that "given a little time, the softening effect of the planting that is just now getting under way will remove at least most of these objections." Through planting, "practically all of the new walls will be concealed and the result will be much more pleasing. However, I know that this is hard to visualize at the present time."[38]

Hugman found it difficult to compromise. When the city recommended he hire a particular landscape architect, he refused on the grounds that it would be a political hiring at too high a salary.[39]

Since Hugman would not shift his emphasis from rock work on his own, Mayor Maverick, who was catching much of the criticism, decided to force his hand by simply cutting Hugman's supply of the offending material. Agreeing with his cousin Rena Green that too much stone may have been used, Maverick wrote her, "In line with your ideas, I have eliminated a large amount that they originally planned to use."[40]

When Hugman found his materials going instead to another project—La Villita—he was furious. Lacking the political instincts that would have helped him deal with the reality of what he was up against, Hugman collected copies of vouchers for the diverted materials and presented them with a protest to Judge Claude Birkhead, one of his original backers and a member of the project's oversight board. To Hugman's dismay, Birkhead, annoyed, asked his chairman, Jack White, to call a board meeting. In March 1940, the board unanimously fired Robert Hugman.[41]

Hugman did not publicly admit his whistle-blowing ploy for another thirty years. At the time he charged instead that he was the victim of "machine politics" for not hiring the landscape architect urged on him by city hall, and he threatened legal action against the city.[42]

For his part, Mayor Maverick explained to the press merely that "work on the project has reached a point where less formal rock architecture and more landscaping with shrubs, trees and flowers is needed." The mayor endorsed Jack White's recommendation of the young architect J. Fred Buenz, a member of the city's park advisory and planning board, to replace Hugman on the project.[43]

Thereafter, work proceeded quietly. The Conservation Society, mollified, swung in to celebrate the project by relocating its October festival from Mission San José to become a River Jubilee. Food stands drew several hundred people to the river's newly landscaped banks around Navarro and Crockett streets, and there was a small river parade.[44]

On March 13, 1941, the Work Projects Administration signed over the completed River Walk to the City of San Antonio. The 21-block effort included 8,500 feet of riverbanks with 17,000 feet of new sidewalks, 11,000 cubic yards of masonry, 31 stairways, and 3 dams, plus some 4,000 trees, shrubs, and plants, and benches of stone, cement, and cedar. The final cost was $442,900, of which $82,700 came from Improvement District bonds and contributions. As many as 1,000 unemployed workers gained jobs. From its berth beneath one of the Mill Bridge's gentle arches, a 16-foot motorboat with pump and hoses began its daily trek to water and maintain the new River Walk.[45]

Wrote Mayor Maverick in his final report: "We believe that in all the United States there is no city in which a river has been made a more attractive resort for all people."[46]

An estimated 50,000 people lined the River Walk on the Monday evening of April 21, 1941, to launch Fiesta Week and dedicate the river project. The main event was the first of what would become Fiesta's grand annual parade of boats sponsored by the Texas Cavaliers, a San Antonio social group established in 1926 to "preserve the Texas tradition of horsemanship in this age of automobiles." The procession left from the Ursuline Academy landing and headed south.[47]

The group's Fiesta king that year, King Antonio XXIII, was George Friedrich, whose Friedrich Company machine shops made a galvanized iron barge for the king. Friedrich commanded a flotilla

of sixty-one otherwise plywood boats. Festooned on the day of the parade with fresh flowers, the boats, without motors, were poled or rowed. A visible link to the Cavaliers' origins came in the next-to-last boat, just before the king's: the king's white horse, which gave the crowd a thrill by tilting the boat when frightened by applause.[48]

Whether the king's horse would fall overboard was not the only concern that night. Another was the fear that a light drizzle would turn into heavy rain. It didn't, but there were plenty of umbrellas in sight as the procession left the Ursuline Academy landing below Municipal Auditorium about 8 p.m., led by a police canoe and followed by a flotilla of paddleboats with masked pilots. A floral American flag adorned the craft of Fort Sam Houston's Third U.S. Army commander, Maj. Gen. H. J. Brees. Sides of one boat were

left
The genius of River Walk planning was in its details, not only in construction elements but in such integrated accessories as plantings, benches, signage, and the variety of lights shown here, many of them not installed or no longer in place.

right
At the Fiesta boat parade dedicating the River Walk on April 21, 1941, King Antonio XXIII— George Friederich— addresses the crowd, while Mayor Maury Maverick and Jack White, in the uniform of the parade-sponsoring Texas Cavaliers, look on.

covered with balloons, occupants of another waved lighted sparklers, and, farther along, hula girls moved only their hands and arms to avoid rocking their boat.[49]

The light rain caused trouble for Victor Braunig's float. Since Braunig headed the power company, his boat was decorated with strings of electric lights, lit by a small generator rigged up on board. But rain seeped into the light sockets, short-circuiting the strings and knocking out the generator. In the confusion of trying to fix it the system's operator fell overboard, and the boat remained dark for the rest of the trip.[50]

Past the Navarro Street bridge the parade reached the reviewing stand, on the steep banks where similar ones happened to have stood for the first river parades in 1905 and 1907. Mayor Maury Maverick, wearing a raincoat, announced descriptions of each craft as it passed. After the boats' journeys of an hour and quarter they began tying up at the Arneson River Theater. Participants disembarked for a reception above, in the newly restored La Villita.[51]

So did Robert Hugman's River Walk end its initial phase, buffeted by unexpected events and left at the end of its course with an appearance slightly different from what was planned. Hugman was no longer on board, his guiding inspiration short-circuited by dis-

One of the newly completed River Walk's signature features was the flagstone walkway around the reconfigured cascade, which poured air conditioning runoff from the nearby Majestic Theater into the river near the present Omni La Mansion del Rio.

agreements with original supporters. The direction of the River Walk and of the nation were about to take an abrupt turn. Yet downtown San Antonio's river was now transformed with a uniform design executed with uncommon flair. And that, as time would prove, was reason enough to celebrate.

7
DISUSE AND RESCUE

As the city and nation turned to focus on fighting World War II, San Antonio's River Walk, dedicated so gloriously in April 1941, became an afterthought. Hardly a dollar materialized of the $5 million that now-dismissed architect Robert Hugman predicted would be quickly invested on commercial projects along the new River Walk. One basement restaurant did open on the River Walk below the Houston Street bridge, but there were no colorful adobe shops, no potters at their wheels, no swans nor water pheasants bobbing on the lazy stream. San Antonio did not become, as the *New York Times* had expected, "the city where you shop from gondolas."

Jack White, who engineered the project, left the Plaza Hotel to operate the newly-formed White Plaza Hotels, with facilities in San Antonio—the former Lanier Hotel, at North St. Mary's and Travis streets—and in Dallas and Corpus Christi. Maury Maverick, defeated for re-election as mayor, shifted his energies to Washington to run the War Production Board's Smaller War Plants Corporation.

Yet threads of continuity remained. Jack White's successor at the Plaza, Tom Powell, maintained the hotel's heavy promotion of its location on the river, though San Antonio's claim to be the Venice of America was scaled back to the Venice of Texas. In October 1941 the Conservation Society put on its second annual River Jubilee/Festival/Carnival and then three more, skipping a war year. In 1947 the event was moved up to La Villita, where it evolved into the immense four-night Fiesta fling now known as A Night In Old San Antonio.[1] The Texas Cavaliers' river parades resumed after the war, joined by a new annual event, the River Art Group's River Art Show, in 1947.

opposite page
A sailor and his girlfriend have the newly completed River Walk to themselves.

left
A gondolier perched on a corner of his craft poles the boat toward the bridge later named for its designer, Robert Hugman.

THE PLAZA HOTEL IN SAN ANTONIO
"The Venice of Texas"

THE PLAZA HOTEL IN SAN ANTONIO, "THE VENICE OF TEXAS"
Beautification of the river in downtown San Antonio has created a unique "River Street" through the heart of the business district. The Plaza Hotel overlooks this fascinating outdoor playground.

City Hall did have a dozen flat-bottomed wooden boats built in mid-1942 on the order of those in Xochimilco, Mexico, but the city had to be prodded to keep up the river's maintenance. Six civic groups complained that lights had gone out and that oil and refuse were being dumped in the river. The motorboat with its pump and hoses fell out of use, but, with the war over and shortages lessening, five parks workers newly assigned to the river watered its banks with hand-held hoses. Stewart King, the city forester, set out to turn the sheltered River Walk—five degrees cooler than street level above in summer and five degrees warmer in winter—into a subtropical botanical garden.[2]

Robert Hugman kept a presence on the River Walk by opening his office in the basement of the turreted Clifford Building next to the Commerce Street Bridge. Jack White hung onto his River Walk boat concession, renting canoes and boats moored beneath Navarro Street's Mill Bridge. He tried adding a fleet of sixteen motorboats, christened with such names as the General Eisenhower and the Lieutenant [Audie] Murphy, for daily trips beginning at 5 p.m.[3]

Uniformed soldiers took girlfriends out in canoes. VIPs floated by, one of them movie actress Rita Hayworth in a procession entertaining wives of Army pilots away on assignment. In spring 1943, Treasury Secretary Henry Morgenthau Jr. was in town to help kick off a national $13 billion war bonds drive as part of the "greatest publicity and advertising campaign" in the nation's history. Crowds gathered around the River Walk at the Houston Street bridge to watch workers representing five divisions of the war bond "army" race on the river in amphibious jeeps.[4]

Boats in a patriotic river parade in 1942 were poled from the marina under Navarro Street's Mill Bridge, top left. The program at lower right features the top prize at the 1948 art show, a statue of King Neptune sculpted by Pompeo Coppini.

In these views from the World War II years, clockwise from top left, J. B. Wicks, assisted by Vernon Poerner, worked on his contract for building ten new river boats; architect Robert Hugman set up his office at the foot of the new stairway from the Commerce Street bridge; an exercise of amphibious jeeps below the Houston Street bridge promoted war bond sales; a boat ride for wives of absent fliers featured actress Rita Hayworth, third from left in the first barge; and, victorious troops were welcomed home with a grand parade down the River Walk.

At the end of the war San Antonio's river may not have changed into a shopping mecca. But it was, no doubt, the nation's only city to welcome its soldiers home not with a ticker tape parade through downtown, but, as the war wound down in July 1945, by feting them on the river in a boat parade through downtown.

The national energy released by the returned veterans and the booming economy did not reach down to San Antonio's River Walk, no matter how hard the city tried to promote it. Tourists admired the River Walk, but did not flock there in sufficient numbers to attract many businesses. Establishing a restaurant at river level was nearly as hard after the redesign as before. A year after its dedication, George Dabalis and Evangelos Sarantakes opened the first business on Hugman's River Walk, the Riverside Sea Food & Steak House, in the Book Building basement space of the mid-1930s Riverside Gardens. A neon sign at the stairway down from the Houston Street bridge announced dining and dancing, canoes, boats, even the route to La Villita, long though the walk may have been. But by 1951 the Riverside Sea Food & Steak House was gone.[4]

It remained for another entrepreneur beside another bridge to open a longer-lasting restaurant on the River Walk. This one, the first commercial venture on the Great Bend, opened in October 1946, due more to the competitive nature of the appliance business than to fervent commitment to the River Walk.

Alfred Beyer owned an appliance store at the southwest corner of Commerce Street and the river, but kept being undersold by the appliance section of Joske's Department Store a block away. Anxious to find supplementary revenue, he built stairs beside his store down to the river. He dug flood-deposited silt from the basement—the lower remnants of a Spanish-era home—and opened it as Casa Rio Mexican Foods.[5]

Soon Beyer got the idea of adding boats. He tried building a gondola, but it "sank like a stone." A swan adorning another—modeled on boats in Boston's Public Gardens—was decapitated by the river theater's bridge, and a barge designed for dining—the S.S. Enchilada—capsized, with diners aboard. But he finally got it right. In 1949 he took over the boat concession, and replaced rental canoes with two-passenger pontoon paddleboats.

Along the San Antonio River, Venice of America, San Antonio, Texas

Photo by Harvey Patteson

above
Jack White gave hat badges to his early River Walk concession boatmen.

left
Postcards in the 1940s promoted San Antonio not just as the Venice of Texas, but as the Venice of America.

Beyer ended up getting out of the appliance business, and family operation of the pioneering Casa Rio, much enlarged, is in the fourth generation.[6]

Meanwhile, public attention had suddenly regressed to flood control. During the night of September 27, 1946, a cloudburst centered ten miles southeast of town dropped rain over northwestern San Antonio with a greater intensity, though lesser volume, than during the flood of 1921. Had the storm been directly over northwestern San Antonio, damage would have been much greater. As it was, four lives were lost.[7]

There was some flooding in downtown San Antonio—water came nearly knee-deep in the lobby of the Plaza Hotel—but that was due more to over-loaded storm sewers than to any cascade from Olmos

Basin, where floodwaters were held back by the dam. The main impact this time was suffered in the western part of town, along San Pedro Creek and its tributaries, Alazan, Martinez, and Apache creeks. Floodwaters there were lower than in 1921, but damage was intensified by overbuilding in the creeks' floodplains.[8]

Some unfinished business obviously remained to be done. This time public funding mechanisms were in place.

The U.S. Army Corps of Engineers spent five years studying and designing an expanded flood control plan along thirty-one miles of the San Antonio River. It would be more than a decade before work was completed. The tributaries of San Pedro Creek at last got their own broad, concrete-based channels. The convoluted bends in the river at McCullough Avenue and at Ninth Street were finally straightened—as Metcalf & Eddy had recommended in 1920—as was another to the south near Roosevelt Avenue. The floodgate at the upper end of the Great Bend was replaced and a tainter gate was built halfway down the cutoff channel in place of the channel's low dam.

The channel through the King William Street area that Mayor C. M. Chambers fought to keep from being paved was not only paved but straightened and made much deeper—over the protests of many residents— and the bend around Pioneer Flour Mills was eliminated altogether. Though boats were still restricted to the Great Bend, riverside sidewalks and landscaping were extended beside the river for one mile to South Alamo Street, around the curve historically known as Sauerkraut Bend for the large number of families of German origin in the neighborhood. Beyond, the twisting course of the river was straightened in a broad new channel far downstream.[9]

Congressman Paul Kilday got so excited when he landed $15 million in federal funding for a key part of the project that he proclaimed the work would end flood damage in San Antonio "for all time."[10]

With all the attention devoted to flood control upstream and downstream, the River Walk was rising to public consciousness only a few times a year, during river parades or art shows or, beginning in 1958, during the Alamo Kiwanis Club's annual summer

Flooding from a severe storm in 1946 disrupted traffic in southern and western San Antonio, as in the scene at far left in the 1300 block of Frio City Road. This resulted in an extended flood control effort that by 1968 included a broad concrete channel through the King William Street area, left, and an extension of the River Walk from downtown.

weekend Fiesta Noche del Rio in the Arneson River Theater. There were the occasional weekend paddleboats and dining barges, but walkways were mostly deserted. While the narrow banks and semitropical plants were well maintained, who wanted to look at the unkempt backs of buildings looming above?

Neglect encouraged owners to encroach on River Walk property. That drew the attention of some watchful new landladies, members of the San Antonio Conservation Society, which had purchased two historic La Villita properties that backed on the River Walk. In 1948 Mayor Alfred Callaghan promised the group that he would keep an eye on things. Two years later, however, on the opposite leg of the Great Bend, came an encroachment so blatant that the Conservation Society rose up as a body.[11]

The proposal slipped in from an investment group innocuously named Endowment Inc. It was all about education, banker Walter McAllister explained to the ladies of the Conservation Society, apparently with a straight face, when they found out about it. St. Mary's Law School students, it seemed, were having trouble finding parking places. The school needed to keep those students in order to justify an appeal to increase endowment. The school had sufficient space to build a parking garage in the rear—overlooking the River Walk—but the garage needed an exit. That, unavoidably, must be a new bridge, only twelve feet wide, over the river to Crockett Street. Of course, customers of nearby businesses could use the garage, too. Yes, the bridge would cross between one of the River Walk's two arching pedestrian bridges and a picturesque

An arched garland similar to those on the boats of Xochimilco was used in San Antonio on the Lupita, stopped near the Arneson River Theater in the 1940s. Another was used on a studio set for San Antonio's first television broadcast, on WOAI-TV on December 11, 1949. Featured on the show was the young singer Rosita Fernandez, right, beginning the noted career that led decades later to the naming in her honor of the theater's bridge as Rosita's Bridge.

cascade, but the new bridge would be higher up, at street level, and any pedestrians or boats wanting to pass could still do so.[12]

Conservation Society members cried foul. They could cast their case with a little sleight of hand, too, and reinvent their origins to fit the circumstances. Sixty-eight members petitioned Endowment Inc. to abandon the project, flatly declaring of the group's beginnings, apparently for the first time, that "the San Antonio Conservation Society was formed twenty-seven years ago to save the downtown river from being covered over and made into parking lots."[13]

Members marched on City Hall. They funded a lawsuit against the city for granting a construction permit. The society asserted that the parking garage would serve a private rather than a public purpose, and thereby violate "the public park and recreation area" along the river. A district judge, however, ruled that the plaintiffs had no standing to file because they would suffer no personal damages from the construction. The decision was upheld on appeal.[14]

By its high-profile if unsuccessful assault on the intrusion, the San Antonio Conservation Society may well have saved the River Walk. The flat concrete bridge did slice across one of the favorite River Walk views, as the concrete bays of the new parking garage gaped from above. But the noisy debate had returned the River Walk to public awareness and suddenly offered hope for its future, now that a formidable

advocate was on watch. Things would not get better right away. But they would not get worse.

What the River Walk needed was another Jack White. In 1959 one happened to emerge in the person of David J. Straus, 37, president of his family's appliance wholesaling Straus-Frank Company and chairman of the Chamber of Commerce's Tourist Attractions Committee. Like White, the well-connected Straus had the clout to get things done, got along well with others, and was committed to long-term involvement.[15]

At a party in 1959, "a bunch of us were sitting around in a bull session," Straus recalled. "At that time the River Walk was off limits to the military; it was

Construction in 1952 of an automobile bridge across to a new parking garage in one of the most picturesque sections of the river led to a public uproar that focused new attention on the River Walk.

Shown at the inauguration of a Casa Rio dining barge are, from left, Casa Rio founder Alfred Beyer, new River Walk advocate David Straus, and Casa Rio's general manager, Johnson Smith. The paddlewheel, however, splashed water on diners and could not be used.

trashy, full of winos, and no one would go down there. And so the subject of Casa Rio came up and they said, 'Boy, it'd be nice if we could have a bunch of things like that. Why doesn't someone do something?'

"And so I got to thinking about it that night. The next morning I went down and called on [Chamber of Commerce president] Walter Corrigan at the chamber office and said, 'Walter, do you remember the conversation last night about the River Walk and why doesn't somebody do something about it? Why don't you appoint me as chairman of a committee . . . and let's see if under the auspices of the chamber we can't do something?' And so he said, 'OK, you're chairman of the new committee.'"[16]

Straus and Harold Robbins, the chamber's manager of tourist advertising and promotion, tried identifying property owners through deed records and called on them in hopes they would fix up their properties. They also called on prospective tenants to put them in touch with property owners. But "we just couldn't get anybody to do anything," said Straus.[17]

As with White two decades earlier, Straus became convinced that an overall plan would pull the situation

out of the doldrums. In 1960 Straus helped persuade the chamber and the city to jointly finance a $15,000 River Walk study by California's Marco Engineering Company, a theme park designer noted for its work on Disneyland. A good contact was a former San Antonio Chamber of Commerce official, James V. McGoodwin, who had gone to work for Marco.[18]

Marco engineers, not surprisingly, found the River Walk "run down and in need of repainting, improved lighting, better housekeeping, police protection, and additional park benches." Their solution was "intensive application of creative design to the selection and arrangement of props and dressings."[19] Translation: Add glitz.

The sixty-page Marco plan recommended incorporating La Villita as the grand entrance to a new River Bend Park. The city should construct and own shops and restaurants along the river, though these "probably would not attract the maximum patronage." What would do that was "considerable show and entertainment" in the form of a River of Fiestas, which within three years should be extended far upstream to Brackenridge Park. Events could range from a Fiesta de Bellas Artes in January to a Fiesta of Parasols in August to a Fiesta de Piñatas at Christmas. Across North Presa Street from Villita Assembly Hall, a plaza for fiestas would be divided by the river and anchored on one end by a replica of the façade of Mission Espada beside a merry-go-round. A water tank near the Arneson River Theater was to be encased in simulated stone for "an authentic ancient appearance."

Since there were only two river-level pedestrian bridges linking opposite shores, Marco planners recommended adding two pontoon bridges that could open to let through barges vending food and souvenirs. [20]

The project was to be overseen by a new city agency, a River Development Board. It could draw 700,000 persons to the River Walk in the first year alone, planners projected, and would yield a sizable profit immediately. The plan was forwarded to city council in May 1961.[21]

Horrified San Antonio architects reacted as if all that was missing were Mickey Mouse and Donald Duck. The noted O'Neil Ford fired off a four-page blast to the Chamber of Commerce charging that "not one man on the city council is trained or able to make a sound judgment on such designs as this holiday play park group of designers are submitting, and they should not have such a responsibility put upon them." He was incensed that such a development would use public land, which he said should be preserved, rather than using only private property, where Hugman and others had intended such development would go. Were favorite public spots going to be

covered with "plaster imitations of Hollywood Spanish architecture?" Ford demanded that a brochure incorrectly implying his participation in the planning be withdrawn from circulation at once.[22]

Disenchantment with the proposal spread. The chamber's Tourist Attractions Committee, headed by Straus, unanimously rejected it as being out of keeping with the city. Marco Engineering's plan ended up in the dustbin, though some of its concepts were remembered for future use.

The uproars over the St. Mary's Law School bridge and the Marco plan had both generated at least as

To get some life into the River Walk, the city and the Chamber of Commerce commissioned California's Marco Engineering Company, planners of Disneyland, to come up with something for San Antonio. The result was considered out of keeping with the city.

DEVELOPMENT OF THE SAN ANTONIO RIVER BEND

MARCO ENGINEERING COMPANY
Wiard Ihnen: *Project Architect*

much heat as light. Each matter would have been less contentious if aided by the input of an appropriate group charged with passing judgment on issues that often were, as O'Neil Ford had indicated, beyond the capabilities of untrained people to decide. Districts in other cities had such advisory bodies, and David Straus thought it time that San Antonio's River Walk had one, too.

Straus and the chamber's Harold Robbins went to Carmel, California, to check out its protective zoning requirements, credited for an aesthetically pleasing city. Then the pair went to New Orleans and visited members of the Vieux Carré Commission, charged with overseeing the historic French Quarter. When they returned, Straus took ordinances of both cities,

As much of its tourism emphasis shifted toward the potential of the River Walk, the Chamber of Commerce moved from the upper floor of an office building to these quarters beside Navarro Street's Mill Bridge.

excerpted the parts most appropriate to the River Walk, added a few of his own, and had attorney Carlos Cadena check the language. The result, approved by San Antonio's city council on March 28, 1962, was City Ordinance 30238. Its purpose was to maintain "the charm and the atmosphere of "old San Antonio" along the River Walk, promote "an integrated shopping, entertainment, and recreation area for visitors," and to create the River Walk Commission.[23]

There were to be seven members of the River Walk Commission, at least two of them "recognized practicing professionals in the field of design and applied arts." Though only an advisory body, it would be the first stop for permits for construction, modification, or painting within the River Bend, as the horseshoe-shaped section leaving and reentering the cutoff channel was being called. All such work was to be "in sympathy with early San Antonio architecture." The commission would also advise city council on property development issues not just within the bend, but also along the rest of the River Walk and the two miles beyond to the headwaters, and in La Villita as well.[24]

The organizational meeting was held on June 1, 1962, at the Chamber of Commerce office. No longer on an upper floor of an office building, the chamber was headquartered on Navarro Street beside the Mill Bridge, on the ground floor with a picture window overlooking the River Walk. There the commission elected investments broker Walter Mathis as chairman. Atlee B. Ayres, who in his 30s as City Plan Committee chairman made early river beautification a top priority and in his 60s scorned Robert Hugman's River Walk design, now became, in his late 80s, a charter member of the River Walk Commission.[25]

Planning began at once for additional entrances down to the River Walk, for promotion, for rules and regulations governing concessions, and for ways to get owners to fix up their properties. In six months the commission had a master plan in the works. The pendulum had swung back to local experts, and the San Antonio chapter of the American Institute of Architects was asked to form a committee to work on the project. The AIA named eight members, headed by Cyrus H. Wagner. As a project title, committee member Ignacio Torres suggested translating River Walk into Paseo del Rio. The term stuck.[26]

Under Wagner's leadership, the architects decided the public River Walk property should be left as it was, enhanced only by further plantings. The focus would be on style of architecture and building materials for commercial and retail development on private property up to street level, and for residential and hotel development above that. Development would be sorted into activity noise zones of quiet (on the bend's southern leg—antique shops, art galleries, and apartments), moderate (on the central leg—a mix of restaurants, shops, and apartments), and loud (on the northern leg—clubs and restaurants). To draw more tourists, a pedestrian link would extend from the Alamo down to the River Walk. The proposal of monthly fiestas was salvaged from the Marco plan, and its attendance projections were cited.[27]

Photographs were taken along the river, a base map was developed, overlays made, drawings sketched, models constructed, and a slide presentation assembled to show civic groups and gain further input.[28]

"In many planning circles during the early '60s," committee chairman Wagner recalled, "it was an accepted fact that people would not walk more than 500 feet to get from one place to another in an urban environment. In order to dispel that 'fact,' I made a cut-out model of the North Star Mall at the same scale as the model and overlaid it on our model. [The mall] extended from the [eastern edge of the bend] to St. Mary's Street, a distance of about 1,400 feet. A slide was made, incorporated into the show, and in our presentations we made a point that people *would* walk well over 500 feet if the

San Antonio's Municipal Information Bureau added an extra bridge at the river theater to dramatize this cover of a 1940s tourism brochure.

walking environment was interesting and pleasant. The slide was always a big hit with audiences."[29]

The unveiling came on April 15, 1963, in a slide presentation by Wagner and Allison Peery to a receptive crowd of civic leaders at Villita Assembly Hall. Two years later the Paseo del Rio plan received a national award from the American Institute of Architects.

As others mulled the plan's implementation, Wagner kept his slide show on the road to all who would hear him. Gradually, individual projects began to emerge. A joint proposal of O'Neil Ford and Allison Peery, with design by Mike Lance, for shops and apartments overlooking the River Walk on South Alamo Street won a national award in *Progressive Architecture* competition in 1963.[30]

Then insurance executive James L. Hayne, who played trombone in a leisure-time jazz combo headed by wholesale grocer Jim Cullum, put together a group

of twenty-two investors to move the musicians into a home on the River Walk. On a deserted section, a 2,400 square foot room in the basement of the Nix Hospital garage was turned into a bistro dubbed The Landing. Two hundred people could sit at its "postage stamp tables." The Happy Jazz Band moved in just in time for Fiesta 1963. It was the first night club on the River Walk, and the first business to open in the Chamber of Commerce's new drive to make the river a highlight for tourists.[31]

Burton Louie's Chinese restaurant Lung Jeu had opened in 1959 on the opposite side of the Commerce Street bridge from Casa Rio, which was beating the odds on the river and staying open, but Lung Jeu survived only a few years. A few doors upstream, Victoria "Mama" Fontana opened her Venice Italian Restaurant in mid-1964 in the basement of the Casino Club Building at the Crockett Street bridge in space formerly occupied by Casa Rio's short-lived western barbecue restaurant. Outside she put up a red neon sign flashing "Pizza." The River Walk Commission, caught unawares, got a sign ordinance through city council. Commission members told Mrs. Fontana she could legally keep her sign since it went up before the new rules, but she agreed to take it down.[32]

As new transformation began to take shape, signage was not the only issue needing to be resolved. While the River Walk Commission began dealing with technical issues to maintain an appropriate visual environment, another group was formed to promote and serve business along the river. This was the Paseo del Rio Association, organized in 1964 by David Straus as a Chamber of Commerce committee soon chaired by James L. Hayne and run by chamber staff member Jimmy Gause.

Then there was the problem of security. Since 1945 the River Walk had been off-limits for military personnel from midnight to 6 a.m., but there were problems during other hours. In 1962 a visiting Air Force colonel made headlines when he was stabbed one evening and robbed of $150 as he walked on a picturesque but deserted section of the River Walk near Pecan Street. A policeman was assigned to patrol the river on a paddleboat, but got "his shoes and pants legs got all wet after one trip." Then the police department bought a twelve-foot flat-bottom boat. It sank on its first cruise. It was raised and a defective drainage plug was fixed, but then the boat wouldn't move; its electric motor wasn't strong enough. Finally the department bought a five horse-power motor, and the police patrol program got under way. "We feel like we've prevented a lot of

By the mid-1960s, things were stirring on the River Walk. At far left, a 1940s gondola dramatized an arrival at The Landing, where a jazz band played in the basement of a hospital building. At near left, around the bend, evening business was brisk at Casa Rio, its dining atmosphere heightened by gas-fed tiki torches on the deserted walk across the way.

disturbances and obnoxious incidents," said Police Chief George Bichsel.[33]

As conditions continued to improve, David Straus gathered other investors, purchased three properties in the heart of the bend, and went searching high and low for tenants. He contacted a friend at a Chicago consulting firm that did work for the Playboy Clubs. Would Hugh Hefner like to put a Playboy Club in one of Straus's properties? San Antonio residents, the military, and convention goers would certainly support one. In Hefner's absence, the response came back that Playboy was more interested in Houston and Dallas. On the central leg of the bend, Straus had Cyrus Wagner design River Square, its initial tenants far more prosaic—a Mexican folk art shop named La Sirena and two restaurants, the Stockman and Kangaroo Court.[34]

Straus credited the upsurge in development of the private property beside the publicly-owned River Walk to developers "having most dealings with property owners rather than working through city government politics." Straus noted, "There's a story behind everything that happened," mostly of businessmen dealing directly with each other, though there were some hybrid situations.

"Poling boats along the river was difficult enough with gondolas because of the mud on the bottom," Straus recalled. "What was needed to move larger groups were larger boats, with motors. I went to Reginald Roberts, an architect who was also a boat

enthusiast, and got him to do some drawings. Then I went to City Council and suggested that they advertise for bids for a boat concession, but the council didn't think the matter was important enough to do anything about it.

"So I had a boat built half the size of the proposed boats, and paid for it myself. I asked Casa Rio to provide food, invited the mayor and council to lunch on board and said, 'This is what I had in mind.' That did the trick. The city advertised for bids, the boats were built, and Casa Rio, which had been running the smaller boats, got the concession to operate them."[35]

The now familiar flat-bottomed, steel-hulled barges, seating up to forty people for sightseeing and twenty for dining, went into operation in 1967 just as a suddenly ambitious business establishment was jump-starting downtown development with plans for nothing less than a world's fair, to open on April 1, 1968. Celebrating the two hundred fiftieth anniversary of the founding of San Antonio, it would key off San Antonio's central location in the Western Hemisphere with the theme Confluence of Cultures in the Americas. Its name would be HemisFair '68. Timing of the new attention to the River Walk and of the safeguards dropped in place to manage its future growth could not have been better.[36]

The site selected, in July 1963, was ninety-two acres in a declining neighborhood immediately southeast of central downtown San Antonio. The last high-rise hotel built downtown had been, amazingly, the Plaza, in 1927. New hotels would be needed, and quickly, not only for fairgoers but for future hordes at a new convention center in a corner of the fairgrounds within sight of the River Walk.[37]

As if that were not good news enough for Paseo del Rio boosters, a new River Walk extension, conceived by O'Neil Ford, would be dug a third of a mile east to a lagoon surrounded by the convention center and its theater. The extension was financed through part of the HemisFair bond issue overwhelmingly approved in January 1964. Fairgoers would ride on river barges. It took a very short

creative leap for developers to realize that if new hotels were built on the River Walk, fairgoers—and conventioneers—could ride the same barges to the hotels, then stroll beside the river to new shops and restaurants.[38]

The problem of getting enough pedestrian traffic to make the River Walk a success was solved.

Two new hotels, both on the River Walk, were built for the fair. The larger was the twenty-one-story, 481-room Hilton Palacio del Rio facing the fairgrounds across South Alamo Street and backing directly on the River Walk below. The hotel seemed hopelessly behind schedule when construction magnate H.B. Zachry took charge. He finished the Hilton in 202 days, barely on deadline, by having individual modular rooms built offsite and furnished down to towels on the racks and soap in the soap dishes, then trucked to the site and lifted into place with giant cranes.[39]

Location of the second hotel came in a roundabout way. While in the Nix Hospital awaiting the birth of his youngest child, St. Mary's University alumnus Patrick Kennedy happened to gaze down on the original St. Mary's buildings, last used by the university for its law school and recently abandoned. They were on the River Walk, the main section was attractive and historic, and there was room for more construction, once the parking garage—and its abhorred bridge across the river—were removed. The result was the 200-room La Posada: The Inn on the River

River Square, a complex of new and restored buildings with upper stories fronting on Commerce and South Presa streets, opened beside a new bridge at the time of HemisFair '68.

Two new hotels, both oriented toward the River Walk, opened for crowds attending the world's fair in 1968. At left, the Hilton Palacio del Rio was finished in time by hoisting fully furnished rooms into place with a crane. At La Posada, later the Omni La Mansion del Rio, a controversial 1950s bridge over the river was jack-hammered away and a parking garage demolished for the expansion of restored 1850s buildings that once housed St. Mary's College.

access, requiring them to be shored up to permit excavations beneath.[41]

A measure of the new respect for the River Walk was the amount of attention from architectural critics during the six months of Hemis-Fair. Ada Louise Huxtable of the *New York Times* spoke for most when she called it "the city's outstanding amenity." Austin architect Sinclair Black, writing in the *AIA Journal*, thought La Mansion del Rio's new rear wall beside the River Walk, "neatly folded in response to the giant cypress trees, serves to define the river space and animate its edge. The scale of the magnificent trees becomes more evident by their proximity to the building."[42]

Walk, soon renamed La Mansion del Rio and, in 2006, Omni La Mansion del Rio. Its renovated four-story, mansard-roofed stone building, built in 1852, was joined by a new wing, likewise dressed in white stucco and enclosing a Mediterranean-style central patio as it extended along the edge of the River Walk.[40]

By the end of 1967, with the fair only four months away, the number of businesses on the River Walk had jumped to ten. Twelve buildings were being renovated so more businesses could open in time for the fair. While most of these buildings opened on the streets above, few had basement levels for River Walk

Black used the Palacio del Rio's "conquistador contemporary" design to make a backhanded but "very valuable point about the strength of the river as an urban design context. To have a measure of success, buildings need not be special or particularly well-designed when located on the river. . . . Even a self-conscious attempt inevitably and fortunately fails to dilute the power of the river space."[43]

With land and funds both scarce, the new 1,650-foot River Walk extension, four feet deep, had to follow a relatively straight course as it was dug twenty-six feet beneath the level of South Alamo Street and cut through the rear of sites of newly razed buildings along the south side of Commerce Street to reach a lagoon enfolded by the Convention Center. Its style followed that of the original River Walk, though it lacked some characteristic nuances. As the concrete-walled dark passage below South Alamo Street emerged to more concrete walls rising starkly above inaccessible landscaped terraces, one writer thought "boating through this extension of the Paseo del Rio seems like being under the ramparts of the Morro Castle."[44]

Morro Castle or not, the River Walk extension would be relandscaped and extended and extended again, as San Antonians traded the challenges of neglect of the River Walk for the challenges of its success.

This view of the main portion of the HemisFair '68 grounds west past the Tower of the Americas shows the River Walk extension coming from the right of the Hilton Palacio del Rio toward far right center, then making a sharp turn into the space between the theater and convention center. The domed arena nearby was later removed for a convention center expansion that extended the River Walk extension.

8
CROWN JEWEL OF TEXAS

Eighty years before the River Walk finally came into its own with HemisFair '68, an anonymous writer predicted that San Antonio's river, developed properly, could one day become the "crown jewel of Texas." For decades the prevailing wisdom dismissed such predictions as "idle dreams." And yet, some thirty years after the fair, that prophecy came true when San Antonio's River Walk for the first time surpassed the Alamo as the top tourist destination in Texas and became a key to the city's annual $7 billion tourism industry.[1]

The River Walk, sensed one writer, is "a trip through a linear paradise of infinitely changing vistas." Concluded another: San Antonio's River Walk "provides an experience that has not been successfully duplicated anywhere else in America."[2]

From throughout the nation and the world—from Japan, China, Peru, Canada, Malaysia—planners come to plumb its secrets. Singapore's Urban Redevelopment Authority studied two riverside developments that were "very different but both strongly tied into their communities"—along the Seine in Paris and the River Walk in San Antonio. In Mexico, Monterrey pumped water back into its long-dry Río Santa Lucía and planted cypresses beside sidewalks lined with tiers of new buildings. "It's supposed to be just like San Antonio," said a Monterrey official. When residents organized to upgrade the noxious setting of New York City's Gowanus Canal, there was no question of where they were headed. The goal was to become, the *New York Times* reported, "Brooklyn's version of the Riverwalk in San Antonio."[3]

When HemisFair closed in October 1968, all the glowing prophecies and "idle dreams" about the San Antonio River seemed suddenly within reach. Conventioneers at the new convention center in the near corner of the former fairgrounds did in fact take boats to the two new hotels along the River Walk, all at once busy with pedestrians. No longer did the river need ad hoc committees nor the periodic alarms of City Beautiful advocates or ladies clubs or Robert Hugmans or Jack Whites or David Strauses to rescue it from neglect or impending doom. Now committees and boards and commissions were essential simply to

opposite page
Making a grand entrance into the Arneson River Theater during the 2006 Fiesta River Parade, sponsored by the Texas Cavaliers, is King Antonio LXXXIV, Rick Shaw.

keep development on course and preserve the distinctive character of the River Walk in the face of relentless success.

To emphasize the new thrust, the San Antonio Chamber of Commerce in 1970 changed its logo to a flowing blue design suggesting the river. Tourism promoters boosted the River Walk with a new campaign, "Forget the Alamo!" The city's River Walk ordinance was updated, expanding the advisory commission's jurisdiction from the Great Bend to the entire two-mile River Walk, even to parts of all buildings "within a visual line from the River Walk area." San Francisco's Skidmore, Owings and Merrill was commissioned for a study, completed in 1973, for guidance on issues ranging from flood control and water quality to housing and social services along an eight-mile river corridor.[4]

With enough businesses along the River Walk to support it, the Paseo del Rio Association, formed as a Chamber of Commerce committee, was spun off as an independent organization under the direction of Claire Regnier. Its former director, chamber staff member Jimmy Gause, joined City Manager Tom Huebner on road trips to land more conventions and river-oriented hotels.

More attention was also being paid to the River Walk's designer, Robert H. H. Hugman, so ignominiously dismissed by the city in 1940 while overseeing completion of the project he had conceived and nurtured. Hugman never again attempted a project of that scope, but quietly did a variety of residential and institutional design work in San Antonio and South Texas, for a few years in association

Among streams around the world inspired by San Antonio's river is the Río Santa Lucía in Monterrey, Mexico, with paddleboats and riverside café and, right, its own river theater.

with Paul G. Silber in the firm of Hugman & Silber. In 1957 he went to Randolph Air Force Base as a project architect, retiring fifteen years later.[5]

Hugman's first public honor for the River Walk did not come until 1970, at a ceremony held by the San Antonio Chapter of the American Institute of Architects. After thirty years of being ignored, he was overwhelmed by the sudden recognition. "When we praised Mr. Hugman for his vision and design, he broke down and cried," remembered architect Boone Powell. "The rest of us stood and cheered."[6]

After that, Hugman occasionally commented on directions the River Walk was taking. Was it becoming "the Venice of America or the Convention Center on a creek?" he asked when he spoke at a River Walk Commission luncheon in 1972. "Lasting good taste, beauty, quiet dignity, satisfying aesthetics, and good food are the things which will perpetuate the river," Hugman wrote River Walk Commission Chairman David Straus a few years later. "Please do not allow these river assets to be eroded. Once they are gone it is too late." He also urged Straus not to approve the proposed paving of the Arneson River Theater's grassed seating. The grass remained. When a parking garage was proposed on the riverside site that later became the location of the Hyatt Regency Hotel, Hugman protested in person to the city council. The parking garage was ultimately built at the northeast corner of Commerce and Presa streets.[7]

Hugman's rehabilitation became complete in 1978, two years before his death at the age of seventy-eight. On behalf of the city, Mayor Lila Cockrell dedicated five bells hung in Hugman's honor in the open arches rising behind the Arneson River Theater stage, where he had originally intended bells to be. Hugman did the first striking. His onetime office sign—"R. H. H. Hugman AIA, Architect"—was later duplicated in his memory in its original location, on the curving outdoor river level of the old Clifford Building beside the Commerce Street Bridge. The sign became, in effect, Robert Hugman's signature on the River Walk project.[8]

Now that it was clear that River Walk use would continue to grow, the aging technical infrastructure regulating the Great Bend needed fine-tuning. In the words of longtime San Antonio River Authority General Manager Fred Pfeiffer, the process would turn the River Walk into "less a product of nature enhanced by man than a product of man enhanced by nature."

A tainter gate in the cutoff channel served as a movable dam to keep the level of water constant in the Great Bend. In keeping the water higher on its upstream side than on the other, the gate had to block the channel. This frustrated riverboat operators and their passengers, for boats reaching either end of the Great Bend were forced to double back. Nor could the gate, adjusted manually, regulate the water level with great precision.

"Water all but covers the sidewalks in some blocks, particularly in the south section of the bend," Paseo del Rio Association Director Claire Regnier complained in 1977 after taking a magazine writer on a tour. "It is difficult to maintain our positive image while 'wading' a guest through a walking tour." She also had to be careful "to avoid walking near those staircases and footbridges which I know to be in a state of disrepair." Until the situations were corrected, she suggested that tours for writers and convention executives be conducted by boat.[9]

Such problems led to bond issue financing of a major overhaul of the downtown river's flood control system, completed in 1988. The tainter gate, moved several

A flood control system completed in 1988 included a new dam at Nueva Street below the Great Bend, replacing an older one and keeping the entire River Walk upstream at a uniform water level.

years earlier to below the bend's outlet into the cutoff channel to permit circular movement of boats, was removed altogether. Water in both the bend and the channel was kept at the same level by a new dam and gate at Nueva Street, a block south of the end of the Great Bend. Just above the dam went a marina for boat storage and maintenance and a River Walk operations center, where the water level along the River Walk upstream was electronically monitored and maintained within a fraction of an inch. With the bend and channel clear of obstructions, boats could at last follow a circular route.[10]

Also, it had been discovered that Olmos Dam, two miles north, was not protecting the city as fully as first thought. An engineering study completed in 1974 praised the "unusually competent attention" to the quality of its concrete and placement, but found that if such storms as those of 1921 and 1946 were to occur directly over the Olmos Creek watershed, the dam could become unstable and topple over. The dam was partially reconstructed, with a spillway instead of a roadway along the top and with correction of other flaws as well.[11]

These improvements were coming just as the city's post-HemisFair promotions began to pay off. San Antonio's first major postfair hotel, the 500-room Marriott Riverwalk, opened in 1979 at the eastern end of the fair's river extension. Its façade served as a visual terminus as the river bent sharply south to enter the Convention Center lagoon.

Ground was broken the same year for a second major hotel, the 633-room Hyatt Regency on the eastern bank of the Great Bend's central leg. Its plain design was praised for making the sixteen-story hotel "surprisingly unobtrusive" in its setting, though others noted that its design did not comply with the city ordinance requiring new River Walk buildings to be "in keeping with early San Antonio architecture."[12]

When the Hyatt opened in 1981, it incorporated a River Walk feature recommended by architects in 1963: a pedestrian link between the Alamo and the river named the Paseo del Alamo. Its entrance was through newly excavated remains of the Spanish mission wall on the west side of Alamo Plaza. Steps descended beside—and beneath—water cascading down a complex of concrete channels symbolizing the city's early acequias. The water flowed into the lower level of the Hyatt to become a major feature of the atrium. From there it appeared to flow through the atrium wall

The Paseo del Alamo opened in 1981 as a pedestrian link between the River Walk and the Alamo, with water features symbolizing San Antonio's early system of acequias.

into a narrow channel extended from the river to the hotel. A transparent pane, however, kept Paseo del Alamo waters within the atrium to be recycled back up to Alamo Plaza. A nearby well, screened by shrubbery, pumped fresh water into the river to maintain water quality.[13]

At its River Walk level, the Hyatt gained a well-known tenant: the Jim Cullum Jazz Band, directed by its founder's son, Jim Cullum Jr., and formerly known as the Happy Jazz Band. It had been playing in the lower level of the Stockman Restaurant since moving from its original Landing in the Nix Hospital basement upstream. From the band's Hyatt location, National Public Radio in 1989 began broadcasting its hour-long "Live from The Landing" to some one million listeners worldwide.

During earlier radio broadcasts on San Antonio's clear channel WOAI, the band promised a record each week to the listener writing in from the farthest distance. "One week we got a letter from Bing Crosby," remembered Cullum. "He said he was listening to the show from a friend's yacht in Acapulco Bay, and he said he hoped he'd get the free record."[14]

The Landing was screened from the outdoors by a glass wall that kept the sound of the music inside, a bow to the increasingly sophisticated regulations of a River Walk besieged, as the world rushed in, with so many new situations challenging its integrity. Wide-ranging guidelines for the likes of building codes, signage, colors, maintenance, and vendors' carts expanded to nineteen pages. Park rangers armed with sound meters patrolled the River Walk to enforce noise control regulations.[15]

Becoming equally complicated was the River Walk's oversight by the San Antonio Parks and Recreation Department, which created titles like "River Operations Superintendent, Horticultural and Environmental," a position charged with overseeing some three dozen workers maintaining what in 2004 had been declared a National Horticultural Landmark for its "magnificent urban ecosystem." This features more than a hundred species of native and tropical plants, ranging from espe-

On the south side of the River Walk extension near the Convention Center, water from a well bringing fresh water into the river appears to be a natural waterfall.

ranza, caladiums, and oleander to gingers, jasmines, brugmansias, and philodendrons to bananas, avocados, and limes. Some 30,000 annuals are planted each year.[16]

Maintaining the river itself became a bit easier in mid-2006 with the debut of Lady Eco, a maintenance barge five years in development. Previously, workers had to scoop out floating debris from dead leaves to foam cups with single long-handled nets. The $100,000 barge, custom designed by John Olthius's San Antonio–based Aqua Sweepers International, features two arms that extend to a combined span of thirty-five feet. Each arm has six detachable nets that skim the water and, when the arms are retracted, can be dumped into a trash bin on board. A crew of three can sweep the river along the entire main River Walk, from the Nueva Street maintenance center to Lexington Avenue, in forty-five minutes.[17]

As word spread about San Antonio and its River Walk, increasing numbers of conventions flocked to the city, filling the new hotels and creating the need for more. The River Walk's extension was extended for a block north under Commerce Street, to enter a lagoon enclosed by that rarest of downtown developments—a new shopping mall, a favorite project of Mayor Henry Cisneros.

"Just add water" was the slogan for the $200 million, ten-acre, million-square-foot Rivercenter Mall when it opened in 1988. The 135 shops, restaurants, and Imax theater on three levels were wrapped in glass—in subtle, blue-based colors—around the new lagoon. A bridge reached an island stage for performances.[18]

Beside the mall rose San Antonio's new tallest building, the thousand-room, forty-two-story Marriott Rivercenter Hotel. It exceeded by eleven stories the Smith-Young Tower, since renamed the Tower Life Building, San Antonio's tallest building since it was built in 1929. The Tower Life Building had kept the title of tallest building longer than any other building

top
National Public Radio has aired River Walk performances of Jim Cullum's Jazz Band on "Live from The Landing" since 1989.

below
Lady Eco, a newly designed maintenance barge, sweeps debris from the river's surface into nets on arms that can swing out to a span of thirty-five feet.

in a modern major American city. The River Walk's impact on the economic growth of San Antonio could hardly have been more obvious.[19]

The River Walk was extended yet again. As part of a $218 million Convention Center expansion, the

The River Walk has led to construction of San Antonio's tallest building, the forty-two-story Marriott Rivercenter Hotel, facing the Rivercenter Mall lagoon reached by an extension of the River Walk extension under a Commerce Street bridge.

River Walk was cut through the lagoon's south wall and extended between the added convention facilities, sometimes obscured by a landscape created to resemble the Texas Hill Country. The lagoon was narrowed to the width of the new channel, providing enlarged paved gathering space on either side. The new extension was bordered with limestone retaining walls and passed over landscaped islets. A cascade flowed into the extension's end from HemisFair Plaza above. The Convention Center project was completed in June 2001 in time for the 25,000 persons arriving for Rotary International's ninety-second convention.[20]

Through it all, San Antonio would end up with the sort of River of Fiestas agenda envisioned by the Marco plan in the 1960s. The oldest event remains a favorite, the river parade first sponsored by the Texas Cavaliers in 1941, which draws some 200,000 spectators each April. The dozen other annual parades, overseen by the Paseo del Rio Association, range from the St. Patrick's Day parade on a river dyed green to a canoe race to a mariachi festival. The year's first event became a Mud Festival, with its own celebrity king and queen, during the channel's annual draining for maintenance. The cleaning has turned up everything from Timex watches—still ticking—to a wedding band—returned to its owner—to the occasional relic from the Battle of the Alamo.[21]

Most dramatic is the holiday parade and lighting ceremony, which draws 150,000 spectators. In August, the Amigos del Rio volunteers' Bulb and Socket Party aids city workers in replacing 120,000 bulbs in strings as long as ninety feet taken down early each year from some 125 riverside trees. A month later, four professional tree climbers, two groundspeople and electricians begin rehanging the lights, ceremoniously switched on the Friday night after Thanksgiving to begin the River Walk Holiday Parade of more than two dozen floats. Two nights later, singers from dozens of school, church, business, and civic groups begin caroling from boats cruising the Great Bend. Some 2,000 sand-weighted bags hold votive candles for the Fiesta de las Luminarias, inspired by the luminarias of Santa Fe, New Mexico, during the first three weekends in December.

At Rivercenter Mall, boats portraying vignettes of the Christmas story float into the lagoon for a pageant. After Christmas, college bands from the Alamodome's Alamo Bowl contestants hold floating pep rallies. The River Walk Holiday Festival concludes on New Year's Eve with entertainment at Rivercenter and strolling musicians, performers, and bands on barges.[22]

During the holiday festival, the Arneson River Theater maintains its role as a River Walk focal point by hosting Saturday afternoon performances by carolers and, at night, Fiesta Navidad del Rio, sponsored by the Alamo Kiwanis Club, also sponsor of the summertime weekend Fiesta Noche del Rio. That event's noted longtime singer Rosita Fernandez was honored near her retirement in 1982 with the naming of the theater's Hugman-designed bridge in her honor. As she starred in the show for twenty-six years, Rosita crossed the bridge to sing favorites of Mexico and Latin America. A Japanese television special on bridges of the world featured that bridge along with such others as the Brooklyn Bridge, London Bridge, and Venice's Bridge of Sighs. Those bridges take people from one side to another, the show reported, whereas Rosita's Bridge unites cultures.[23]

A highlight for the Arneson River Theater came in 1984, when it was the setting for Bizet's opera *Carmen*,

Rivercenter Mall, opened in 1988, has 135 stores and shops on three levels around a River Walk lagoon.

jointly produced by the Berlin Opera and the short-lived San Antonio Festival. The San Antonio Symphony played the accompaniment from barges anchored in front of the stage. Some actors arrived onstage from boats rounding the Great Bend. When Carmen was killed, the actress playing her was thrown into the river. She surfaced around the bend, out of sight.

With the seemingly unending numbers of pedestrians and conventioneers and events coming to the River Walk, a problem of only a few years before had been reversed. Then the difficulty was getting pedestrians from busy Houston Street down to the uncrowded River Walk. Now the challenge became getting pedestrians from the busy River Walk up to

the uncrowded Houston Street, where a major commercial revitalization was under way.

One effort to get people up to the street was the construction, in 2002, of an elevator and stairway at the North Presa Street bridge, with an arrow pointing conspicuously up to Houston Street. Near the Commerce Street bridge, an elevator reaching a trolley bus stop likewise doubled as River Walk access for the handicapped. A third elevator, masquerading as a clock tower, was built at Crockett Street. Below Crockett Street, Robert Hugman had designed a picturesque series of stone arches to shelter small shops, in the manner of stalls along the Seine. The arches were finally built in 1988 and opened thirteen years later as entries to an underpass beneath Crockett Street to a complex of restaurants and shops in the basement of Aztec on the River, the former 1926 Aztec Theater.[24]

Nor did there seem to be an end to new hotels opening onto the River Walk. Some could incorporate historic River Walk features. The Valencia, on the river at Houston Street, detached the 1918 Riverside Restaurant balcony from the building, which was demolished, and preserved it just below its original location as the outdoor Acenar Restaurant's Maverick Balcony. The Contessa, at Navarro Street's Mill Bridge on the site of the parking lot that replaced Nat Lewis's mill, preserved in its lobby a concrete WPA-built bench moved to make way for the hotel's entrance to the river. The luxury Watermark Hotel and Spa across from the Omni La

Mansion del Rio was to be built inside the walls of the onetime Frank Saddlery Company Building that fronted on Commerce Street. After the old building's streetside façade collapsed during reconstruction, the rear wall was taken down and the Watermark was built within new walls closely resembling those of the earlier building.[25]

Smaller developments were fitting into vacant or underused space as well. South Bank, a three-story cluster of new brick buildings in a late-nineteenth century style, eliminated two street-level parking lots inside the sharp northeast corner of the bend. Its tenants included a Hard Rock Cafe, County Line barbecue restaurant, and Starbucks Coffee. To the

An arched wall designed by Robert Hugman to enclose stalls for shops was finally built in 1988 and cut through beneath Crockett Street in 2001 as entrances to the Watermark Hotel and Spa and the shops of Aztec on the River in the former Aztec Theatre building.

south, another cut into a former parking lot produced the five-story Presidio Plaza, anchored by Planet Hollywood.

By 2005, concerns were being raised as fully one-third of the restaurants on the main River Walk had become chain outlets common to strip malls throughout the country. Landry's, which already operated a Landry's Seafood House and a Joe's Crab Shack on the River Walk, gutted the 1895 Chandler Building at the Crockett Street bridge for a Rainforest Café that opened in 2006.

Robert Hugman's concern over whether the River Walk would be "the Venice of America or the Convention Center on a creek" had become quite real. "Obviously, the mystique, the uniqueness, the ambience of the River Walk pulls them into this," Paseo del Rio Association Director Greg Gallaspy observed of the chains.[26]

Justin Arrechi was more outspoken. The ice cream company he established on the River Walk in 1981 was one of three locally owned businesses ousted from the Casino Club Building to make room for a Landry's Saltgrass Steak House. Of the new Landry's Rainforest Café Arrechi complained, "it's filled with fake rocks, fake trees, and howling monkeys. It's just not right." Jim Cullum Jr. gathered more than 6,500 signatures on a petition to limit chain outlets on the River Walk.[27]

Landry's chief Tilman Fertitta responded. "This is my business. I started it," he said of the company with 38,000 employees at 311 restaurants in thirty-six states. "I don't think of myself as this big corporate chain."[28]

Mayor Phil Hardberger disagreed with Fertitta's self-assessment, and determined to keep the River Walk from looking like "a shopping mall in Minneapolis or New Jersey." He put the city attorney to work on an ordinance based on San Francisco's limiting of "formula restaurants," those sharing such characteristics as names, signage, menus, and staff uniforms with nine or more restaurants under the same ownership.[29]

This was not the first clash between the city and River Walk business owners. The question of who owned rights to the River Walk itself had flared up in 1998, when the city sued owners of four restaurants who refused to pay more than $1 million in back rent for placing revenue-producing tables on what the city claimed was public right-of-way. The restaurant owners responded with deeds dating from Spanish land grants that they said proved their ownership of property rights to the edge of the river. But to which edge? Did construction of the River Walk move the legal edge of the river to the water's new edge, or did the legal line remain where it was before the River Walk was built? And just where, by the way, was that?[30]

The city, for two centuries having had little economic impetus to explore the issue, settled out of court. The restaurant owners surrendered their title claims in return for lower rents and lease options longer than those for other owners, plus more of a voice in how rental revenues would be spent. One such use was increased attention to careful restoration of original River Walk elements, a project overseen in 2006 by FisherHeck architects Lewis S. Fisher and Charles John.[31]

The city had already reaffirmed its right to control navigation of the river. Whom the city would choose to do the navigating became the subject of headlines in 1995, when one million tourists a year were being ferried on the stream. A fiercely sought ten-year contract valued at $40 million was awarded not to the Beyer-Lyons family that had the concession since 1949, but to Yanaguana Cruises. The new concessionaire replaced the fleet of noisy gasoline-powered

barges with thirty new barges run by compressed natural gas, not only quiet but giving off no strong fumes. After a subsequent dispute over payment of commissions, however, the contract was transferred to JoAnn Boone's Rio San Antonio Cruises. By the time Rio San Antonio won renewal of the contract, its fleet was up to forty boats, Rio Trans taxi service had expanded from nine stops to thirty-nine, and the contract's value was estimated at $120 million.[32]

Business deals soaring into nine figures were plain signs that the River Walk was something people wanted more of. The River Walk expansion south through the King William Street area to Pioneer Flour Mills remained isolated, since the dam at Nueva Street kept boat service from being extended. The original upper portion of the River Walk—the nearly one mile from the Great Bend north toward Municipal Auditorium— also had little commercial development. A signal for the potential of its residential development had, however, come in 1979, when a group led by David Straus completed the Left Bank Condominiums across from the restored Ursuline Academy buildings, later the

During construction of the Valencia Hotel on the site of the restaurant building built by George M. Maverick, the tile-roofed balcony added over the new river park in 1918 was removed and reinstalled at a slightly lower position as the Maverick Balcony of the Valencia's outdoor Acenar Restaurant.

campus of the Southwest School of Art and Craft. The upper River Walk became even more attractive some twenty years later, thanks to completion of another engineering tour de force, one more enormous than the flood control project of the 1920s.

Since construction of Olmos Dam, the main river channel and its bypass of the Great Bend had been critical for flood control. Much of downtown remained classified as within a flood plain, sometimes making building permits difficult to obtain. Outside the Great Bend, no permits were given for construction at the river level, and usually not at a level lower than eighteen feet above the River Walk. After 1997, that problem changed dramatically. Downtown San Antonio was no longer considered as within a flood plain, and River Walk developments outside the Great Bend could build patios as close as eight feet above the River Walk, near enough to lend a much better sense of being on the River Walk.

That year marked completion of a flood tunnel 24 feet in diameter, some 150 feet below downtown San Antonio. It began just south of Brackenridge Park at Josephine Street and ended three miles south at Roosevelt Park, an elevation 35 feet lower than the entrance. Just west of downtown, a similar, one-mile tunnel carrying San Pedro Creek floodwaters from Quincy to Guadalupe streets was completed in 1989 with few problems.

Both the San Pedro Creek and San Antonio River tunnels were known as inverted siphon tunnels. They could carry approximately half of the runoff from a hundred-year flood. Though its construction was mainly underground and out of the public view, like the 1920s project it had its own delays, dramas, and frustrations, and grew into a ten-year

Residential development along the upper River Walk includes the Left Bank Condominiums, built in 1979 near the North St. Mary's Street bridge.

In 1987, a gigantic boring machine began the eleven-year project that drilled a three-mile flood control tunnel beneath central San Antonio.

effort that tripled estimated costs to $111 million.

The U.S. Army Corps of Engineers began work on the river tunnel in 1987. For this one workers also used a 620-ton, laser-guided tunneling leviathan nicknamed "The Mole." As it ground through the earth, The Mole placed pre-cast concrete segments in rings one foot thick.

But less than 500 feet from its start at the southern end of the river tunnel, fractured shale formations caved in, dropping fragments larger than the machine could grind up. The Mole got stuck 150 feet below the Brackenridge High School girls' gym. Workers dug a vertical shaft 900 feet ahead, then tunneled back to

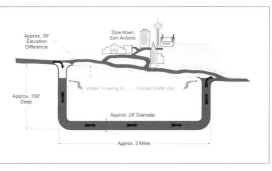

clear the fallen shale. It took a year to get it free.

Only eighteen months after the river tunnel was completed, up to twenty inches of rain on October 17, 1998, brought flooding that claimed eleven lives in low-lying areas and caused more than $120 million in property damage, much of it to the east in Salado Creek's drainage area. Most of the city's 1.2 million residents, however, were unscathed, as decades of flood control efforts paid off. The new tunnel carried as many as three million gallons a minute, leaving minimal damage in the city's central core.[33]

Another payoff came as officials realized that the tunnel could also recycle water. Riverflow down-

In these views along the upper River Walk, clockwise from top right, workmen in 2001 rebuild deteriorated walls in a project that also paved the river bottom, transformed a parking lot at Augusta and Convent streets into a park leading down to the river, and buttressed a retaining wall near Municipal Auditorium with a faux-wood concrete trellis designed by Carlos Cortés. Water at Pecan Street's Weston Centre cascades to the level of the River Walk and is recycled.

stream at the tunnel's exit could be diverted into the tunnel's outlet shaft. It could then be pumped from the upstream inlet shaft and sent back down the river. Wastewater pumped from treatment plants to the tunnel's inlet was added. Three pumps in Brackenridge Park previously sent five million precious gallons of drinking-quality water daily into the river downtown. The pumps were no longer needed.[34]

By this time the city was facing the consequences of deferred maintenance of the upper River Walk, as structural failures were causing some walls to collapse. With prodding from Mayor Howard Peak, a $12.5 million overhaul began in 2001. Water was drained from the upper channel for more than a year as the bottom was paved, providing a solid footing for those channel walls rebuilt with matching stonework. Remaining walls were reinforced, the channel's west side walkway was completed, and a parking lot

far left
Potential damage from a severe storm in 1998 was minimized by the new three-mile flood tunnel, its terminus at Roosevelt Park shown discharging stormwater into the river's downstream channel.

left
Helping integrate the cutoff channel into the River Walk is Portal San Fernando, which links the river with Main Plaza and San Fernando Cathedral, seen through the trees at left of center.

at Augusta and Convent streets was converted into a small park, with steps and a ramp descending to the River Walk. A section of a retaining wall was buttressed by a faux-wood trellis of concrete trees by artisan Carlos Cortés. Beneath bridges, mosaic tile murals were done by Oscar Alvarado.[35]

One striking new feature of the upper River Walk had been the cascade recycling from the street level of the 30-story Weston Centre down to the river level. Now, as smaller hotels and developments crept into the area, the Weston enlarged its waterfall area with new plazas on either side.[36]

As the tunnel's completion helped spread new development upstream, so did creativity at last flow to the once unsightly cutoff channel. In 2001 the river's long-recommended link with Main Plaza materialized in the form of the Portal San Fernando, a park designed by Lake/Flato Architects with symbolic water features descending from Main Plaza to the river, a design that used an estimated two hundred tons of limestone. A zigzag walkway cantilevered over the west side of the cutoff channel extends from the park over newly placed small islands to meet the main River Walk at the beginning of the Great Bend.[37]

Diagonally across the channel, the new Drury Plaza Hotel in the former Alamo National Bank Building picked Sprinkle Robey Architects to design a $3 million walkway along the eastern edge of the cutoff channel to connect the walk at each end of the bend, a walk not cantilevered but built up from the

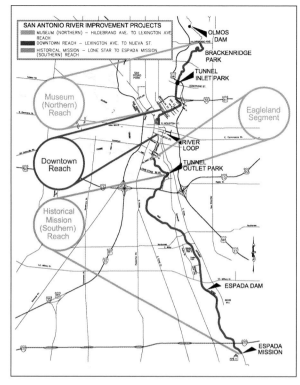

channel's base. No longer would pedestrians have to climb to street level to reach the opposite end of the Great Bend. A bridge across the channel was also planned.[38]

Beyond both ends of the River Walk, projects exceeding earlier imaginings were beginning to take shape with planning for a $174 million, ten-year River Improvements Project. Guiding its planning and execution was the San Antonio River Oversight Committee, formed in 1998 and co-chaired by former Mayor Lila Cockrell and architect Irby Hightower. Charged with raising $15 million in private funds for amenities under a separate, thirty-year arts master plan was the San Antonio River Foundation, formed in 2005 under the presidency of former Conservation Society President Sally Buchanan and the directorship of Gayle Spencer.[39]

The River Improvements Project—designed by Houston's SWA, a nationally recognized firm of landscape architects—will, in effect, make the River Walk more than six times longer. It is broken into two main segments, each emphasizing flood control, environmental restoration, new amenities, and recreation.

The four-mile segment of the river from the northern end of the River Walk past the San Antonio Museum of Art and Witte Museum up to Hildebrand Avenue was dubbed the Museum Reach. The Museum Reach was to capitalize on nearby commercial and residential development potential. The southern, nine-mile section was named the Historic Mission Reach, as that portion of the river passes the four eighteenth-century Spanish missions—Concepción, San José, San Juan, and Espada—that form San Antonio Missions National Historical Park. Hike-and-bike trails were planned along a route restored to replicate the original functioning of the river—straightened, partly paved, and stripped of vegetation and natural landscape during the flood control project of the 1960s and 70s.[40]

The environmental portion of the Mission Reach project will restore the functioning of the river, rather than its precise original path, using the arcane discipline of fluvial geomorphology. The straight, concrete rubble-based channel is being replaced with soil-based meanders similar to earlier ones, reducing erosion and, with the replanting of native trees, grasses, and plant life, drawing wildlife back to the area.[41]

Remarked the U.S. Army Corps of Engineers district commander, Col. John Minahan, at the groundbreaking for the section above the Mission Reach—the Eagleland Segment—in 2004: "Twenty-two years ago, if you'd told me I'd be standing here in San Antonio taking a perfectly good flood-control project and putting it back the way we found it, I'd probably [have said], 'That's not possible.' "[42]

However far north or south the walk was extended, there seems little doubt that the heart of the River

Pedestrians will be able to complete a circuit of the Great Bend without having to go up to street level thanks to this walkway along the eastern wall of the cutoff channel, shown under construction in 2006.

Walk would remain in downtown San Antonio, the crucible of its halting evolution for more than a century. There, its narrow banks twenty feet below the level of the streets, its noises hushed by the denseness of cypress trees towering above and the wealth of exotic plants thriving in the sheltered climate, the San Antonio River Walk creates its magical sense of mystery, anticipation, movement.

Reflected sunlight and shade dance on the rippling waters. The muffled clatter of plates carried to a colorful blur of riverside tables mingles with the spicy aroma of the servings. Well-worn walkways squeeze past diners and wind on, uninhibited by railings as they curve around bends and slip beneath bridges framing new scenes. Small barges glide quietly by,

their passengers' heads swiveling in unison to follow the pilot/guide's narrative in words hardly audible to pedestrians a few feet away. A tiny island with its own cypress tree is a favorite spot for small weddings, using a symbolic iron altar placed there in honor of the Franciscan priests who named the river in 1691.

From their expressions, many of those wandering the River Walk seem transported to another dimension, and they're trying to figure out which one. The mix of buildings looming discreetly through the trees says "city." But can this timeless setting really be San Antonio? Is this the Venice of Texas? The Venice of America? Aragon? Romula?

The River Walk could be all of these yet is not quite any of them. The episodic swings between attention and neglect, between conflicting master plans and none, of natural setting vs. Disneyland, have layered San Antonio's River Walk with a unique sense of spontaneity, yielding a work that may remain forever precarious and unfinished, yet one that stands as a triumph of enterprise and human imagination.

Passersby can happen upon weddings on an island with a symbolic iron altar commemorating the naming of the San Antonio River in 1691. The islet is reached over a tiny bridge near the Hotel Contessa.

For more than a century the scene has been changing near the four-story Clifford Building at the Commerce Street bridge. In 1902 the banks of the river, top left, crossed by a picturesque iron bridge, were overgrown and unkempt. The city came up with a wider concrete bridge and beautified the banks, still well kept in 1935, if deserted, top right. The WPA's River Walk project provided sidewalks and new landscaping, and by the 1950s tourist gondolas, lower left, were floating by. By the early twenty-first century the solitude was gone, as effects of the world's fair that built the tower visible to the left of the Clifford Building vaulted the River Walk into position as the top travel destination in Texas.

ACKNOWLEDGMENTS

Many sleuths have provided valuable information and assistance for this book. Among them are Rich Mansfield, corporate librarian for the engineering firm of Metcalf & Eddy in Wakefield, Massachusetts; Carole Prietto, archivist at Washington University's Olin Library in St. Louis, which holds the records of San Antonio's first professional city planner, Harland Bartholomew; photo archivist Tom Shelton of the University of Texas at San Antonio's Institute of Texan Cultures; San Antonio Conservation Society Librarian Beth Standifird; Dianne Hart at San Antonio's Department of Parks and Recreation; and Mike Bratten at the San Antonio River Authority. Victor Darnell of Kensington, Connecticut, retired chief engineer of the former Berlin Bridge Company, provided material on San Antonio's historic iron bridges.

Others who have been of particular assistance include Maria and Fred Pfeiffer, Sharon Bray, Sally and Bob Buchanan, Mary Ann Delmer, Thomas Ewing, Irby Hightower, Sarah W. Lake, Bill Lyons, Scott Martin, Boone Powell, Douglas Steadman, and David Straus, plus my usual support team—my wife, Mary, and our sons, William and Maverick.

★

PHOTO CREDITS

Architectural Record 42

A Comprehensive City Plan for San Antonio 86, 87

Victor Darnall 13

Daughters of the Republic of Texas Library at the Alamo 23 (left, Schuchard Collection), 114 (lower left)

Rosita Fernandez 118 (left)

Lewis F. Fisher cover, ii, 1–5, 7–11, 12 (left), 15 (right), 16, 18–22, 24, 27, 29, 32 (below), 33–38, 39 (above), 40, 41, 43, 49 (right), 50–53, 54 (top left and below), 55 (below), 56, 57 (right), 58 (top left and below), 59 (left), 64, 65, 67, 77, 80, 81, 84, 85, 90, 91, 93, 97 (left), 98, 99 (left), 100 (left), 101, 102, 104, 109–13, 114 (right), 115, 116 (right), 117, 118 (right), 119, 122, 123, 124 (left), 125, 127, 129, 132, 133 (right), 134, 136, 137 (above), 138, 139, 142–44, 146, 147 (left), 149–51

Ford, Powell & Carson 135

Fort Sam Houston Museum 58 (top right),

Frees & Nichols Inc. 74

From Dawn to Sunset 39 (below)

C. H. Guenther & Son Inc. 15 (left), 68 (left)

Hall S. Hammond 55 (top left)

Patrick Kennedy 128 (right), 141 (left)

Bill Lyons 116 (left)

Mike Osborne 141 (right), 147 (right)

Paseo del Rio Association 140

Roberto Perez, *La Prensa* 130

Maria Watson Pfeiffer 46

Metcalf & Eddy 47, 48, 49 (left)

San Antonio Conservation Society x, 78, 82 (right), 83, 96 (left), 97 (right), 99 (below), 103, 105 (left), 108 (left), 133 (left)

San Antonio *Express* 25, 30, 31, 32 (above), 68 (right), 73

San Antonio *Light* 28

San Antonio *News* 70

San Antonio Parks & Recreation Dept. vi, 137 (below)

San Antonio River Authority 44, 145, 148

San Antonio's River 95

David Straus 124 (right)

The Trail 59 (right), 60, 61

University of Texas at San Antonio Institute of Texan Cultures 12 (right), 17 (below, Ellen Schulz Quillin Collection), 54 (top left), 69 (San Antonio *Express-News* Collection), 79 (above, courtesy Mrs. R. H. H. Hugman), 82 (left, courtesy Frank W. Phelps), 105 (right, courtesy Robert H. Turk); San Antonio *Light* Collection 62, 66, 76, 79 (below), 88, 89, 92, 96 (right), 99 (above right), 100 (right), 106, 108 (right), 114 (top left); Zintgraff Collection 120, 121, 128 (left)

Witte Museum 6, 14, 23 (right), 55 (top right), 57 (left)

NOTES

Preface

1. Emily Edwards to Peggy Tobin, May 25, 1966, letter in Conservation Society Library. For a more complete account of the matter, see Fisher, *Saving San Antonio*, 210–11.

1. San Antonio's River

1. Olmsted, *A Journey Through Texas*, 150.

2. Sidney Lanier, "San Antonio de Bexar," in Corner, *San Antonio de Bexar*, 91.

3. Harriet Prescott Spofford, "San Antonio de Bexar," *Harper's*, 835

4. Stothert, *Archaeology and Early History*, 70; *Express*, "San Antonio River Assumes," Oct. 15, 1905, 17. Its springs usually dry for the past century, the headwaters area, now on the campus of the University of the Incarnate Word, is listed on the National Register of Historic Places as the Source of the River Archaeological District. The area is scheduled for ecological restoration.

5. A variety of terms has been used to describe the river's major downtown bend—Big Bend, Horseshoe Bend, River Bend, River Loop, Great Bend. (Paseo del Rio refers to not just the bend but to the entire River Walk.) Big Bend, however, is the name of a national park in West Texas. It is a horseshoe bend, but, more accurately, a sideways horseshoe bend. It is not the only river bend, as a few of the many original river bends still exist, and river loop sounds like a highway. This book therefore uses an early term that seems to work best at many levels: Great Bend.

6. Cox, *The Spanish Acequias of San Antonio*, 3–6. San Antonio's double-arched stone aqueduct built to carry Mission Espada's acequia across Piedras Creek remains in use, part of the most complete Spanish irrigation system still operating in the United States.

7. The foundry declared a nuisance was built in 1876 at the corner of Market and Presa streets and moved to the eastern edge of downtown, where it grew into Alamo Iron Works. The site was later used for the Carnegie Library. San Pedro Creek supplied lesser amounts of water for commercial use, chief among them a soap works set up on its west bank at Martin Street by a German immigrant, Johan Nicholas Simon Menger.

8. McDowell, "San Antonio's Mills on the River." On Feb. 12, 1899, the river itself froze for the first time in thirty years. This put an ending to the ribbing of one Fort Sam Houston lieutenant by his fellow officers. The lieutenant had brought ice skates from his previous assignment in Montana to semitropical San Antonio, but he skated that day in triumph on the San Antonio River. The river has not frozen since. (*Express*, "Brig. Gen. Rochenbach Returns," Sept. 11, 1928, 11.)

9. Fisher, *C. H.Guenther & Son*, 24, 27. C. H. Guenther & Son has maintained that location while growing into a national food conglomerate, the oldest such one in the nation continuously run by the same family.

10. *Light*, "When Boats Dotted," May 22, 1910, 8; *Express*, "History of City Long Linked," Dec. 31, 1933, 7-C. A noted contemporary of Blankenship was "a Pennsylvania Dutchman named Bender," who had a furniture store near the river at Commerce and Presa streets. "So fond was Bender of fishing in the river," one writer reported, "that when the spirit moved him he closed up his store, hung a sign out, 'gone fishing,' and until he returned to his store he was to be found along the banks of the river pulling in large trout and perch." (*Light*, "San Antonio in Olden Days," July 10, 1910, 30.)

11. *Light*, "Fishing for S. A. Pearls," July 12, 1937, 3-A.

12. Newcomb, *The Alamo City*, 54; *Express*, "History of City Long Linked," Dec. 31, 1933, C-7. In the 1730s, a pedestrian bridge across Commerce Street helped those crossing from the San Antonio settlement to Mission San Antonio de Valero/the Alamo. In 1786, Francisco Calaorra received a Spanish land grant on present-day Crockett Street in return for using his boat as a public ferry at that crossing. (WPA, *Along the San Antonio River*, 21.)

13. Maria William James, *I Remember* (Charles Albert Sloane, comp., San Antonio: The Naylor Company, 1938), in Steinfeldt, *San Antonio Was*, 222.

14. Crystal Sasse Ragsdale, *The Golden Free Land: The Reminiscences and Letters of Women on an American Frontier* (Austin, 1976), 169, in Steinfeldt, *San Antonio Was*, 222.

15. Arda Talbot, "Beautiful Homes of Bexar County," *Bexar County Homes and Cookery* (San Antonio, 1937) in Steinfeldt, *San Antonio Was*, 222.

16. *Express*, "History of City Linked, Dec. 31, 1933, 7-C.

17. *San Antonio Express*, Sept. 18, 1883, in Everett, *San Antonio: The Flavor of Its Past*, 57.

18. Ferdinand Roemer, *With Particular Reference to German Immigration and the Physical Appearance of the Country* (Oswald Mueller, trans., Waco: Texian Press, 1967), 124–25, in Steinfeldt, *San Antonio Was*, 216.

19. *San Antonio Ledger*, July 28, 1853; *Express*: "Bathing in the San Antonio River," July 30, 1911, 17; "History of City Long Linked to Winding River," Dec. 31, 1933, 7-C; "Two Are Here," Aug. 23, 1936; Bushick, *Glamorous Days*, 44.

20. *Express*, "Nymphs at Natatoriums," Aug. 15, 1895, in Everett, *San Antonio: The Flavor of Its Past*, 57; *Express*, "Bathing in the San Antonio River," July 30, 1911, 17.

21. Bowen's Island, actually a peninsula, was called an island through a technicality. It was surrounded on three sides as the westward-bound river ended the Great

Bend by sharply turning south and doubling back on itself to go east before heading south again. An overflow channel of the Concepción Acequia cut across the peninsula's narrow connection to land, thus making the peninsula, when water was high and the overflow channel was in use, a piece of land surrounded by water. Two successive straightenings of the sharp loop firmly tied Bowen's Island to adjacent land. It is remembered by a historical marker on the site.

22. Knight, "The Cart War," 322; San Antonio City Council Minutes, OL-9, May 8, 1851, p. 20.

23. "Nymphs at Natatoriums" in Donald Everett, *San Antonio: The Flavor of Its Past*, 57; Richard Everett, "Things In and About San Antonio," 102.

24. Richard Everett, "Things In and About San Antonio," 103. The San Juan and Espada Mission acequias south of town, however, survived, run by cooperative companies of farmers to irrigate fields. Clean water spared the city devastating cholera epidemics like the one in 1866 that killed nearly 300 residents. The former reservoir is used as an amphitheater in the San Antonio Botanical Garden.

25. Santleben, *A Texas Pioneer*, 129. In 1885 the iron bridge over Houston Street was replaced with a stronger span and moved to Grand/Jones Avenue, where it remained until replaced by a concrete span more than forty years later. (*Light*, "When Boats Dotted," May 22, 1910, 8; *Express*: "Twenty-Three Bridges," Aug. 19, 1911, 18; "Bridge Built in 1870 Still in Service," Nov. 4, 1927, 8.)

26. The South Presa Street Bridge is apparently the Berlin bridge that originally crossed Market Street two blocks away, replacing South Presa Street's wooden bridge when Market Street was widened in 1925.

27. "San Antonio, Texas," "Berlin Bridges and Buildings," 126–27. A typical Berlin bridge in San Antonio was 100 feet long with a center concrete roadway thirty feet wide. Eight-foot-wide sidewalks were on either side of the main trusses, which curved to a midpoint height of some 15 feet. There were decorative posts some 15 feet high at each corner, topped with a finial, as those remaining on the Augusta Street bridge. Retired bridge company official Victor Darnell knew of no other bridges with decorative posts made by the company. (Victor Darnell, Kensington, Conn., to Lewis F. Fisher, interview, Nov. 15, 1996.)

28. *Express*, "'Letters of Gold Bridge' Moved," Dec. 16, 1925. Overhead supports arching between the side trusses had to be high enough so the supports would not clip the tops of the tall floats already common in San Antonio parades.

29. *Express*: "A Steamboat for San Antonio," Sept. 18, 1889, 4; "Sunday Scenes," Jan. 26, 1903, 2; "History of City Long Linked," Dec. 31, 1933, 7-C; *Light*, "When Boats Dotted San Antonio River," May 22, 1910, 8.

30. *Express*, "Rise of River and Creeks," Sept. 18, 1921, 1-A. The sometimes reported depth of waters of nine feet within the church were termed "almost incredible" by later engineers, who did agree that the floodwaters of 1819 reached "a very remarkable height." (Metcalf & Eddy, "Report to City of San Antonio," 12.)

31. *Express*, "Rise of River and Creeks," Sept. 18, 1921; Metcalf & Eddy, "Report to City of San Antonio," 7, 12–13.

32. Metcalf & Eddy, "Report to City of San Antonio," 12–13; Albert Maverick, "Notes on the Flood of 1921," in author's collection.

33. A meeting on the subject was held years later, in 1868, in the wake of the flood of 1865. Another, in 1866, sent floodwaters as high as six feet on streets near the river. (Corner, *San Antonio de Bexar*, 155; "The Deluge," *Daily Herald*, Sept. 1, 1866, 3.)

34. Ibid; "Report of G. Sleicher, F. Giraud and V. Considerant" in Metcalf & Eddy, "Report to City of San Antonio," 327–36.

35. Corner, *San Antonio de Bexar*, 133; McDowell, "San Antonio's Mills." The Concepción Acequia was reopened downstream by connecting it with the Alamo Acequia. The Nat Lewis mill, lacking waterpower, was forced to close, though it reopened later with steam power. More than a half century later, a Boston engineering firm studying San Antonio flood control praised the 1865 engineering report, "in view of the small amount of information available and the paucity of hydraulic knowledge generally at the time," as being "remarkable for its intelligent grasp of the situation and for the breadth of view shown in the measures recommended." (Metcalf & Eddy, "Report to City of San Antonio," 3.)

36. *Express*, "Low State of the River," Aug. 23, 1887, 5.

37. *Light*, "The San Antonio River," Aug. 18, 1887, 4. Moving sewage downstream was another problem, for the *Light* counted more than 200 privies discharging their contents into the river. It termed the river "not an open sewer" but "an obstructed sewer." San Antonio's first municipal sewage system was authorized in 1894 and completed in 1900. (Ewing, "Waters Sweet and Sulphurous," 13 n.9.)

38. Ewing, "Waters Sweet and Sulphurous," 10–11.

39. Ewing, "Waters Sweet and Sulphurous," 12; Morrison, *The City of San Antonio*, 101. Soon after, the Crystal Ice Company purchased its major competitor, the San Antonio Ice Company on Losoya Street, and increased the combined daily capacity to 65 tons of ice.

40. McLean, *Romance of San Antonio's Water Supply*, 9–10. Within three years, eight more wells were drilled at Market Street. To make fuller use of the capacity of his two upstream pump houses, underused since decline of the headwaters, a well was drilled near the upper pump house and three more near the lower one. Making the 1891 strike were Brackenridge-backed drilling brothers Moses Campbell Judson, later Water Works superintendent, and John William Judson, beginning their long careers in South Texas drilling. (Ewing, "Waters Sweet and Sulphurous," 13; David P. Green, *Place Names of San Antonio, plus Bexar and Surrounding Counties* (San Antonio: Maverick Publishing Company, 2002), 55.)

41. Sibley, *Brackenridge*, 102, 141–42; *Express*, "Will the River Run Dry?," Oct. 26, 1922, 8-A. Ownership of the headwaters was still a painful subject for many.

Although granted to the city by the King of Spain, the city council sold them in 1852 to none other than a city alderman, James Sweet, over the strenuous objections of City Engineer Francois Giraud and others. Sweet sold the property in 1859 to a buyer who sold it ten years later to Brackenridge's mother. In 1899 Brackenridge's company donated to the City of San Antonio 320 acres of riverside land south of his estate at the headwaters, which became the nucleus of Brackenridge Park.

42. Sibley, *Brackenridge*, 141.

43. *Express*, "The San Antonio River," Aug. 23, 1887, 7.

2. Building the River Park

1. T. U. Taylor, "The Water Powers of Texas," U.S. Geological Survey Water Supply and Irrigation Paper (1904), 105, in Ewing, "Waters Sweet and Sulphurous," 16.

2. *Express*: "To Beautify The City's River," July 4, 1900, 5; "Sunday Scenes On The San Antonio River," Jan. 26, 1903, 2.

3. *Express*, Feb. 27, 1903, 1, 7.

4. *Express*: "Old Spanish Manner," Sept. 4, 1904, 11; "San Antonio River Assumes," Oct. 15, 1905, 17.

5. *Express*: "Rivercleaning Gang," Aug. 18, 1904; "Citizens Stop Ruin," Aug. 20, 1904.

6. *Express*, "City May Enjoin," July 15, 1905, 10; Phelps, "Shading the Future," 112. The report on the cypress trees was made by George M. Braun, a nephew of Adolph Schattenberg, who had told him of the deal with Adolph's nurseryman grandfather, Gustav Schattenberg. As a child, Gustav Schattenberg helped gather the saplings from farms adjoining the Guadalupe River and transport them by wagon to San Antonio. Braun put the date at "1899 to 1900 or so," leaving sufficient leeway to peg the date at 1904, when Ludwig Mahncke was put in charge of San Antonio River landscaping.

7. *Light*, "Landing of King Selamat," Apr. 25, 1905, 5; *Express*: "Greatest Carnival," Apr. 25, 1905, 5; "San Antonio River Assumes Ancient Importance," Oct. 15, 1905, 17. The king, David J. Woodward, was in a line of kings then designated "Selamat," tamales spelled backwards.

8. *Express*, "Memorial Day Fittingly Observed," May 31, 1905, 5.

9. *Express*: "Venetian Carnival," Apr. 20, 1907, 6; "Canoeing on the San Antonio River," 4.

10. *Light*: "All Are Glad," Apr. 19, 1910, 1; "Civic Pageant An Object Lesson," Apr. 19, 1910, 4; "River Illumination," Apr. 23, 1910, 5.

11. *Express*: "Public Wants River," Feb. 20, 1910, 3; "Plans For Improving River," Mar. 20, 1910, 1-A; *Light*: "Work Starts," Mar. 27, 1910, 26; "River Illumination," Apr. 23, 1910, 5. Also being beautified were the quarter-mile from the northern Navarro to Augusta street bridges, a stretch of 600 feet newly terraced beside the Ursuline Academy and the area below the new St. Mary's School on St. Mary's Street.

12. Farmers along the two surviving acequias south of town fell to quarreling over what little water there was. It took a court to decide that since the Spanish water grant for the San Juan Acequia was dated one day before that for the Espada Acequia, 60 percent of the river's water would be diverted to San Juan and 40 percent to Espada. (*Express*, "Water Rights Settled," Nov. 16, 1911, 16.)

13. *Express*, "Urges Sanitation Now," Aug. 12, 1910. The writer, A. D. Powers, noted that when he arrived in San Antonio he was surprised that his rent was so low for what seemed like "such a splendid place." "I know now why the rental was small," he wrote. "The property is on the San Antonio River. At night when the wind stops blowing it is impossible for us to forget that we live on the 'beautiful' San Antonio River. It stinks to heaven, but I don't imagine it smells like anything in heaven—it would rather remind you of the other place."

14. Wilson, *The City Beautiful Movement*, 1–5, 302–305. By the turn of the century, many middle- and upper-middle-class Americans thought the ideal city to be an ordered whole in which "dignified, cooperative citizens of whatever station or calling" moved in beautiful surroundings, which in turn enhanced worker productivity, improving the economy.

15. Booth, Johnson, and Harris, *The Politics of San Antonio*, 12–13; *Express*, "Final Rally," Feb. 4, 1911. Callaghan defended his stand by stating that the city's growth was about to stop, and that the city should not overextend itself with costly obligations. From 1910 to 1920 San Antonio's population nevertheless grew another 67 percent, to some 161,000, continuing the strain on municipal infrastructure.

16. *Express*: "Citizens Pitch," Oct. 19, 1910, 1; "Final Rally," Feb. 4, 1911; "Mayor Gus Jones' Death Shocks City," Apr. 8, 1913, 1.

17. *Express*: "Commission Charter Defeated," Feb. 5, 1911, 1; "Returns Are Canvassed," Feb. 7, 1911, 18.

18. Coppini, *From Dawn to Sunset*, 176–177; *Express*: "Billboard Men Complain," Oct. 14, 1911, 16; "Ordinance Is Criticised," Dec. 25, 1911, 16; "Coliseum Site," May 4, 1913, 5-B; "Workers Are For City Federation," May 27, 1913, 9; "Clean-Up Pictures," June 7, 1913, 20; Bartholomew and Associates, "A Comprehensive City Plan for San Antonio," 225.

19. *Light*, "Beautifying of City," Mar. 12, 1911, 33.

20. *Express*: "Start the Big Idea," Feb. 5, 1911, 1-A; "The Big Idea," May 18, 1913, 1-A.

21. *Express*: "Start the Big Idea," Feb. 5, 1911, 1-A; "Will Improve The River," Sept. 27, 1911, 11; "The Big Idea," May 18, 1913, 1-A.

22. *Light*: "Francis Bowen Suggests," Feb. 27, 1903, 4; "Fought Riot On Bridge," June 26, 1910, 7.

23. A 1905 graduate of the Massachusetts Institute of Technology, Simpson had returned to his native San Antonio, helped organize the Alamo Canoe Club on the

river, and in 1909 formed, with his brother Guy, an engineering and construction firm that gained much distinction. Simpson had built one of his own two cedar-framed, canvas-covered canoes to paddle the six miles from Brackenridge Park to the Arsenal Street bridge when the river was up. (*Express*, "Canoe Fleet," Sept. 20, 1908, 24; "Canoeing on the San Antonio River," *The Passing Show*, July 27, 1907; Steadman, "A History of the W. E. Simpson Company," 1.)

24. W. E. Simpson, "Report On The Design Of A Conduit" in Metcalf and Eddy, "Report to City of San Antonio," 143–150.

25. *Express*: "Public Baths," Aug. 6, 1911, 15; "Will Improve The River," Sept. 27, 1911, 11.

26. *Express*: "Pump Will Be Installed," Sept. 30, 1911, 16; "City Employees Will Receive," Oct. 3, 1911, 5; "Start Pump Saturday," Oct. 6, 1911, 11; "Snags Will Be Removed," Oct. 8, 1911, 10-A; "For Improving The River," Dec. 29, 1911, 14.

27. *Express*: "Start Pump Saturday," Oct. 6, 1911, 11; "Water Pumped," Oct. 9, 1911, 12; "Million Gallons Pumped," Oct. 12, 1911, 13; "River Is Slowly Rising," Oct. 14, 1911, 16; "River Is Underground," Oct. 18, 1911, 5.

28. *Express*, "Irrigation Ditches Dry," Oct. 22, 1911, 39-B.

29. *Express*: "City Employes Will Receive," Oct. 3, 1911, 5; "Mayor Is Willing," Oct. 24, 1911, 5; "For Improving The River," Dec. 29, 1911, 14; "For Clearing The River," Feb. 12, 1912, 12; "Rates For A New," Feb. 20, 1912, 7.

30. *Express*, "Make City Beautiful," Sept. 1, 1912, 1.

31. Ibid. In a city that would eventually promote itself as unique in America, San Antonio's only unique aspect emphasized for improvement at this time was its river, although existence of the Spanish missions and other attributes were acknowledged in tourist brochures. Preserving those resources would be mostly ignored until the San Antonio Conservation Society arose to defend them a decade and a half later, though such assets continued to dwindle even afterward. In contrast to the general complexities with which cities the size of San Antonio had to deal were those of Santa Fe, N.Mex., with barely 5,000 residents the nation's smallest city with a City Beautiful plan. Its forward-looking chamber of commerce promoted Santa Fe as not just another City Beautiful but as the "City Different." Without the municipal pressures of such far larger cities as San Antonio, its planners could deal with parks, boulevards, and billboards while unifying around Santa Fe's "most priceless possession, an individuality, which raises us above hundreds of American cities." Santa Fe's Plan of 1912 promoted a style based on a study of the city's old architecture and came up with the Spanish names for its original streets, a feature officials didn't get around to labeling in San Antonio for more than another half century. (Chris Wilson, *The Myth of Santa Fe: Creating a Modern Regional Tradition*. Albuquerque: University of New Mexico Press, 1997, 122–23.)

32. *Express*, "Refuse In River," Sept. 20, 1912.

33. *Express*, "Free Bath House," Sept. 2, 1912, 1.

34. *Express*, "Plan To Change," Sept. 6, 1912, 14.

35. *Express*, "San Antonio River," Sept. 8, 1912, 1.

36. *Express*, "To Build River Promenade," July 11, 1915, 1-A.

37. Wilson, *The City Beautiful Movement*, 260; *Express*: "Council Provides," Sept. 4, 1912, 16; "To Write Parts," Sept. 7, 1912, 16; "Refuse In River," Sept. 20, 1912; "To Invite City Planner," Oct. 4, 1912, 7; "Will Raise Fund," Oct. 19, 1912, 5. Two other leading planners were considered, Frederick Law Olmsted Jr. of Boston and John Nolen of Cambridge, Mass. The committee also sought the advice of Chicago architect Marion West, who was doing work in Galveston. (*Express*, "City Plan Meeting," Jan. 21, 1913, 11.)

38. *Express*: "Surkey Seeks To Restore," June 27, 1913, 18; "Building Surkey Seawalls," Aug. 16, 1913, 16; "Surkey's River Beautiful," May 20, 1915, 25.

39. *Light*, "Bowen's Island," Mar. 22, 1912, 3; *Express*, "Bowen's Island Measure," Feb. 4, 1913, 9. In return for title to the old riverbed, the would-be developer of the park—which was never built—donated land for widening both South St. Mary's and West Nueva streets, built sidewalks and curbs along both streets, and absolved the city from any damages incurred in the process.

40. *Light*, "Sans Souci-Coliseum Stock," Apr. 21, 1912; *Express*: "Shorten The River," Oct. 29, 1912, 11; "Suggested Canal," Oct. 30, 1912, 16; "Coliseum Site," May 4, 1913, B-5. The favored site for the coliseum was changed from the Bowen's Island amusement complex to the northern bend, where, when that bend was finally straightened, Municipal Auditorium was built instead of a coliseum.

41. *Express*: "Mayor Gus Jones' Death," Apr. 8, 1913, 1; "Faults Of City," May 31, 1913, 1.

42. *Express*: "Victory For Brown," May 14, 1913, 1; "Bond Issue Will Not Be Greater," May 31, 1913, 1; "Bond Issue For $3,350,000," June 3, 1913, 1; "Surkey Seeks To Restore," June 27, 1913, 18; "Building Surkey Seawalls," Aug. 16, 1913, 16; *Light*, "A Fortune Spent," Nov. 19, 1914, 15. Commerce Street, the city's historic main commercial artery, had been losing business to the broader, parallel Houston Street to the north. Most of the vintage stone blocks were already dressed and needed no further cutting when recycled. In 1917, retaining walls were extended north of the Ursuline Academy with stones from San Antonio's first high school, then being razed. (*Light*, "Extend River Walls," Feb. 5, 1917.)

43. Ellsworth, *Floods in Central Texas*, 10.

44. *Express*: "Farmers and Railroads," Oct. 2, 1913, 1; "Overflow Water Fills," Oct. 3, 1913, 7.

45. *Express*: "River on Rampage," Oct. 2, 1913, 2; "Fire Chief Used," Oct. 3, 1913, 5; "Four Drown," Oct. 3, 1913, 7.

46. *Express*, "Four Drown," Oct. 3, 1913, 1, 7. In one of the more unusual rescue ef-

forts, a wire netting was stretched above the dam forming West End Lake (now Woodlawn Lake) to keep hundreds of fish from being swept downstream. (*Express*, "Saving the Fish," Oct. 12, 1913, 2.

47. Ellsworth, *Flooding in Central Texas*, 1.
48. *Express*: "Loss Small," Dec. 5, 1913, 2; "Militiamen's Good Work," Dec. 5, 1913, 5; "Effects of Flood," Dec. 6, 1913, 3.
49. *Express*: "Loss Small," Dec. 5, 1913, 1; "Damage Is Not Great," Dec. 6, 1913, 3.
50. *Express*: "Loss Small," Dec. 5, 1913, 1; "The Reason," Dec. 6, 1913, 1; "Rail Service," Dec. 6, 1913, 3; "Today's Express And Its Dress," Dec. 7, 1913, 1.
51. *Express*: "Loss Small," Dec. 5, 1913, 1; "Tries to Swim Stream," Dec. 6, 1913, 3.
52. *Express*, "Gray Is Coming," Dec. 7, 1913, 1; *Light*, "Gray Has No Plan," Jan. 11, 1914, 1.
53. *Express*: "Loss Small," Dec. 5, 1913, 1; "Flood Carries Away," Dec. 6, 1913, 3.
54. Coppini, *From Dawn to Sunset*, 205.
55. Ibid. The Indian figure was donated to the city by the San Antonio *Express*. The city planned to fund the statue of Jones, but family members objected to the use of public funds, believing the statue should be funded instead with donations by private citizens. The statue of Jones was never cast, and the northern alcove has remained empty, its sides later removed for entrances to stairs to the River Walk. The four pilasters with lights were removed several years later. The Indian's hand-held fountains did not flow for long.
56. *Light*, "It Will Be Called," Nov. 19, 1914, 16; *Express*, "Commerce Street Is Dedicated," Nov. 22, 1914, 4-B; Carl Moore and Claude Aniol, "75th Anniversary Historical Report," in *The Wheel*, vol. 88, no. 36, San Antonio, Rotary Club of San Antonio, Mar. 8, 2000. The iron Commerce Street bridge was reassembled downstream to cross Johnson Street. During river widening a half century later, it was dismantled along with the Sheridan Street bridge and placed in storage. But workmen sent to scrap the Sheridan Street bridge destroyed the old Commerce Street bridge instead, destroying all but one of its spires and a few fragments. The footbridge now crossing Johnson Street has at its corners the surviving spire and three new duplicates. (Carolyn Peterson, "Letter to the Editor," *San Antonio Conservation Society News*, Nov. 1994.)
57. San Antonio Chamber of Commerce, *San Antonio*, 3.
58. Coppini, *From Dawn to Sunset*, 204; Booth and Johnson in *The Politics of San Antonio*, 13–14; *Express*: "San Pedro Park Has Water," Aug. 18, 1913, 12; "Spring Is Flowing," Aug. 26, 1913, 5.
59. *Express*, "Lends Touch of Beauty," Mar. 10, 1918, 12-A. The addition was made by the estate of the late George M. Maverick, developer of the south side of that block of Houston Street.
60. Frary, "The River of San Antonio," *Architectural Record*, April 1919, 380–81.

3. The Flood of 1921

1. Unisys Weather, "1921 Hurricane/Tropical Data for Atlantic," http://weather.unisys.com/hurricane/atlantic/1921/index.html.
2. Metcalf and Eddy, "Report to City of San Antonio," ii, iv, 112a.
3. *Express*: "Walls Pierced By Openings," Dec. 9, 1913, 1; "Expert's Report Shows Olmos Dam," Dec. 10, 1913, 1.
4. *Express*: "Straighten-River Plan Idle Talk," Dec. 7, 1913, 4-B; "Not A Doubt Of Safety Of Dam, Says Pancoast," Dec. 12, 1913, 1.
5. *Express*, "Flush Gates Are Closed," Dec. 11, 1913, 5. A week after the December 1913 flood, the city sealed gates from the river into the old Alamo Acequia at the northern edge of the city and removed the small dam to limit flooding in adjacent neighborhoods along River Avenue, now Broadway.
6. *Express*: "City May Build Retaining Walls," June 12, 1917, 18; "Condemnation Of Soledad Property," July 24, 1917; San Antonio City Commissioners Minutes, Book B, 467–468, 514.
7. *Express*: "$3,950,000 Bond Issue Election," Jan. 24, 1919, 1; "Bond Issue Approved," July 26, 1919, 1; "City Designates Auditorium Site," June 1, 1920.
8. Metcalf & Eddy, "Report to City of San Antonio," 2–3, 135–137.
9. Metcalf & Eddy, "Report to City of San Antonio," ii, 25, 105.
10. Metcalf & Eddy, "Report to City of San Antonio," ii, 27, 53, 122–134. Of the six cutoffs recommended, four were north of downtown: below Josephine Street, saving 1,200 feet; Ninth Street, 2,450 feet; above McCullough Avenue, 950 feet; and above Navarro Street, the cutoff already planned for Municipal Auditorium, 1,495 feet. South of downtown, a fifth cutoff at Durango Street would save 670 feet and the sixth, above South Alamo Street, would save another 285 feet, while two nearby dams would be removed and tributary channels modified.
11. Metcalf & Eddy, "Report to City of San Antonio," iii–iv, 4, 42–44, 135; *Light*: "Would Cut Out Big Downtown Bend," June 18, 1920, 11; "River Project To Be Started," Nov. 5, 1920, 10.
12. Metcalf & Eddy, "Report to City of San Antonio," 32, 109. Also, bridges needed to be reconstructed or replaced, since barriers could be formed by trestle-style bridges whose trusses caught debris in floodwaters and became dams. Some built at angles to the river deflected floodwaters into the city, and those on piers narrowed the channel.
13. *Light*, "River Project To Be Started," Nov. 5, 1920, 10.
14. C. H. Guenther & Son, Inc. to Mayor and Commissioners, Nov. 27, 1920, and Feb. 10, 1921, letters in archives of C. H. Guenther & Son, Inc., San Antonio, Texas; *Express*, "River Will Have," Mar. 13, 1921, 1-A.
15. *Express*, "River Will Have," Mar. 13, 1921, 1-A.
16. *Express*: "City-Wide Protest Greets Plan," Apr. 1, 1921, 13.
17. Metcalf and Eddy, "Report to City of San Antonio," ii, iv, 112a.

18. Bartlett, "The Flood of September, 1921," 357.

19. *Light*, "37 Bodies Found," Sept. 10, 1921, 1; *Express*, "Known Flood Dead," Sept. 11, 1921, 1; Bartlett, "The Flood of September, 1921," 357; Ellsworth, *Floods in Central Texas*, 9–11.

20. Ellsworth, *Floods in Central Texas*, 36–37; *Express*, "Known Flood Dead," Sept. 11, 1921, 1.

21. *Light*, "37 Bodies Found," Sept. 10, 1921, 1; *Express*, "Known Flood Dead," Sept. 11, 1921, 1; *New York Times*, "40 Known Dead," Sept. 11, 1921, 1. As word about the *Light*'s connection got out, people lined up to plead with the newspaper to send out messages to their relatives on the Associated Press wire.

22. *Express*, Sept. 11, 1921, "Millions Damage Done," 1; Albert Maverick, "Notes on the Flood of 1921," author's collection.

23. *Express*, "Millions Damage Done," Sept. 11, 1921, 1.

24. *Express*, "Known Flood Dead," Sept. 11, 1921, 1; *Light*, "38 Bodies," Sept. 11, 1921, 1; "Soldiers and the Flood," *The Trail*, Sept. 16, 1921, 3.

25. *Light*, Sept. 10, 1921, "37 Bodies Found," 1; *Express*, "Known Flood Dead," Sept. 11, 1921, 1. Another dog awoke a household on Alazan Creek in time for them to escape from floodwaters. Six months later that dog was to lead the Humane Society in a parade. (*Express*, "Dog That Saved Lives," Mar. 22, 1922, 7.)

26. *Express*, "Property Loss," Sept. 11, 1921, 4; *New York Times*, "40 Known Dead," Sept. 11, 1921, 1.

27. Bartlett, "The Flood of September, 1921," 357; Ellsworth, *Floods in Central Texas*, 5, 9–10.

28. Ellsworth, *Floods in Central Texas*, 11.

29. *Express*: Sept. 11, 1921, 1: "Millions Damage Done," "Civilian Shot;" "Soldiers and the Flood," *The Trail*, 3.

30. *New York Times*, "40 Known Dead," Sept. 11, 1921, 1.

31. Ellsworth, *Floods in Central Texas*, 5; *Express*, "Millions Damage Done," "Known Flood Dead," Sept. 17, 1921, 20; Bartlett, "The Flood of September, 1921," 358. Ellsworth's breakdown of the total shows 15 deaths on San Pedro Creek near South Flores and Mitchell streets, 10 on San Pedro Creek between West Commerce Street and the mouth of Alazan Creek; 20 on Alazan Creek between West Commerce Street and the mouth of San Pedro Creek; 3 on Apache Creek between Elmendorf Lake and South Brazos Street near Tampico Street; 3 on the San Antonio River at Newell Avenue; and 1 south of San José Mission. Ellsworth put the total known dead from the storm throughout Texas at 224, including 159 along the Little River and San Gabriel River in Williamson and Milam counties.

32. *Express*, "Laborer Returns," Oct. 14, 1921, 2.

33. *Express*: "2,000 Victims," Sept. 11, 1921, 1; "$18,000 Is Given," Sept. 12, 1921, 1; "One More Street," Sept. 17, 1921, 20.

34. *Express*: "Millions Damage Done," Sept. 11, 1921, 1; "New Week Ushers Fight," Sept. 12, 1921, 1; "Rest Sector During Flood Clean-Up," Oct. 2, 1921, 12-A; *Light*, "Property Loss," Sept. 11, 1921, 4; "Soldiers and the Flood," *The Trail*, 3, 13. "It was the first real chance the soldier had to become acquainted with San Antonio," observed the Second Division's weekly magazine, *The Trail*, in a souvenir flood edition. "The days of the war, with patriotism at fever heat, seemed restored. Business men and gentle ladies missed no chance to get the sentry at his post a glass of cooling refreshment or to place their cars at the disposal of any man in uniform who needed 'a lift.' There was a smile and a kindly word for them all."

35. *Express*: "Known Flood Dead," Sept. 11, 1921, 2; "$18,000 Is Given," Sept. 12, 1921, 1.

36. *Express*, "San Antonio Able to Care," Sept. 12, 1921, 2.

37. Ellsworth, *The Floods in Central Texas*, 5; *Express*: Sept. 12, 1921, 1: "New Week Ushers Fight," "Business as Usual," "Water Should be Available," "Street Car Crews Run;" Bartlett, "The Flood of September, 1921," 361.

38. *Express*: "Cleanup And Reconstruction," Sept. 12, 1921, 1; "Streets Will Be Cleared," Sept. 16, 1921, 20; "One More Street Open," Sept. 17, 1921, 20; "City Prepares To Resurface," Sept. 20, 1921, 20; "Only Two Blocks Remain Closed," Sept. 20, 1921, 20; "Lasting Streets Built," Apr. 18, 1922, E-5; "Streets Soon Will Lose Flood Traces," Oct. 9, 1921, 4. Over the strenuous objection of City Engineer D. D. Harrigan, North Flores Street property owners convinced the city to advertise for bids for old-style wooden paving blocks for streets on which substantial portions of such blocks remained. Harrigan relented when the property owners agreed to pay for any costs beyond those of using the more modern blacktop materials being used elsewhere. (*Express*, "N. Flores Favors," Oct. 7, 1921, 9.)

39. *Express*: "Emergency Food Distribution Ends," Sept. 22, 1921, 22; "Lasting Streets Built," Apr. 18, 1922, E-5.

40. *Express*: "Homes To Get Salvaged Lumber," Sept. 16, 1921, 20; "Immigrants' Son Recalls Prejudice," Sept. 11, 2005, 1-K; "Here Is Your Chance!!," *The Trail*, 1.

41. *Express*, "San Fernando's Congregation Will Dedicate," Oct. 22, 1921, 22.

42. Ellsworth, *Floods of Central Texas*, 1.

43. Bartlett, "The Flood of September 1921," 358, 368.

44. *Express*, "Flood Restoration," Oct. 17, 1921, 1. Attitudes began to change six years later, after flooding on the Mississippi, the nation's worst natural disaster until the New Orleans flood of 2005, left more than one million people homeless. The Flood Control Act of 1928 began the shift to public shouldering of responsibility for causes and effects of natural catastrophes.

45. Bartlett, "The Flood of September 1921," 366.

4. Taming the River and the Great Bend

1. *Express*, "Realtors To Tell," Oct. 9, 1921, 5.

2. The "Letters of Gold Bridge" in Brackenridge Park is believed to be the last lenticu-

lar arch bridge surviving in Texas. (Baker, *Building the Lone Star*, 273.) Just north of downtown, a wide concrete bridge went in at Jones Avenue, where the city's first iron bridge, moved there from Houston Street in 1885, was dismantled. To the south, the badly damaged concrete bridge on South Alamo Street was raised, leveled, and reinforced with a new foundation. (*Express*: "Public Improvements," Apr. 18, 1922, E-7; "Letters-of-Gold Bridge," Dec. 16, 1925, 8; "San Antonio, City of Bridges," Feb. 5, 1928, 1-A.)

3. *Express*: "Public Improvements," Apr. 18, 1922, E-7; "30th Bridge," Apr. 25, 1922, 13; "Rains Hamper," June 18, 1922, 5. North Presa Street was already scheduled to get a steel bridge, the first span at that location. Once the final bridge at Navarro and Crockett was completed, North Presa's temporary bridge would be replaced with a final one.

4. *Express*: "City To Build," Mar. 12, 1922, 12; "Public Improvements," Apr. 18, 1922, E-7; "Bridge at Navarro," Dec. 12, 1922, 9. The "new" Mill Bridge is sometimes compared with the Seine's Pont Neuf, with which it bears a passing resemblance. No architect can be linked with the present Mill Bridge. Bridges then were usually designed by the contractor doing the work. In this case that was the company headed by San Antonio's versatile Charles Terrell Bartlett, a noted hydraulics, irrigation, and structural engineer who also prepared the definitive paper on the 1921 flood, so it can be assumed that the designer was a talented, anonymous engineer in Bartlett's firm.

5. Fisher, *Saving San Antonio*, 82; *Express*, "New Week Ushers Fight," Sept. 12, 1921, 1.

6. *Express*, "Retention Dam To Protect City," Sept. 22, 1921.

7. *Express*, "Property Owners Will Be Asked," Sept. 17, 1921, 1, 20; "Three Methods," Oct. 9, 1921, 14.

8. *Express*: "Survey Of Olmos," Sept. 27, 1921, 7; "Three Methods," Oct. 9, 1921, 14. Three businessmen and four engineers were named to a Flood Prevention Committee to focus on the matter. The businessmen were attorney Harry Rogers, banker Franz C. Groos, and department store owner Nat Washer. Engineers were W. B. Tuttle, Edwin P. Arneson, Willard Simpson, and Clinton H. Kearney. Ex-officio members were Mayor Black, Bexar County Judge Augustus McCloskey, Col. Edgar Jadwin of the U.S. Army Corps of Engineers at Fort Sam Houston, City Engineer D. D. Harrigan, and Chamber of Commerce President Morris Stern. (*Express*, "Property Owners Will Be Asked," Sept. 17, 1921, 20.)

9. *Express*, "Property Owners Will Be Asked, Sept. 17, 1921, 20.

10. *Express*, "C. F. Crecelius Recommended," Aug. 24, 1924, 8.

11. *Light*, "American Military Engineers," Oct. 19, 1925, 1; *Express*, "Olmos Detention Dam," Dec. 12, 1926, 26.

12. *Express*: "Engineer Begins Studying," Sept. 3, 1924, 20; "River Channel Work," Jan. 9, 1926, 1; "Work Begins," Jan. 12, 1926, 4; "2,100-Foot River Bend," June 1, 1926, 6.

13. *Express*: "Two Bends," June 8, 1926, 8; "Old Mill Wrecked," Aug. 19, 1926, 5.

14. *Express*, "City Buys River Channel Land," Mar. 16, 1926, 9.

15. *Express*: "Ornamental Fountains," Oct. 26, 1924, 2; "River Lighting Ordered," June 9, 1926, 24; "Three Plans," June 16, 1926, 9; "River Lighting," July 3, 1926, 20.

16. Fisher, *Saving San Antonio*, 3–8; *Express*, "Queen's Pageant on River," Nov. 13, 1924, 11. In the puppet show, San Antonio's unique aspects were represented by six golden eggs. The river was a subcategory of the egg marked "Beauty."

17. Fisher, *Saving San Antonio*, 183–84.

18. *Express*, "$175,000 Voted," June 15, 1926, 1.

19. *Express*: "New Channel To Cost $250,000," July 14, 1926, 7; "Flood Channel Waits," July 30, 1926, 6; "Overflow Channel Plans," Jan. 13, 1927, 5; "Street Will Top," July 2, 1927, 6; "50 Foot Channel, Crecelius," Oct. 18, 1927, 11; "City Will Rent Channel Lots," Nov. 20, 1927, 11.

20. *Express*: "Flood Channel Plans," June 23, 1927, 22; "Street Will Top," July 2, 1927, 6; "Mayor Outlines Plans," Aug. 9, 1927, 8.

21. *Express*: "Section of River Cut-Off," Sept. 27, 1927, 24; "Wider Overflow Channel," Oct. 2, 1927, 8.

22. *Express*: "Section of River," Sept. 27, 1927, 24; "Wider Overflow Channel," Oct. 2, 1927, 8.

23. *Express*, "City Will Not Change Plans," Oct. 11, 1927, 8.

24. *Express*: "50 Foot Channel," Oct. 18, 1927, 11; "Contract Let For New Channel," Oct. 20, 1927, 22; "Work On Cut-Off Channel," Jan. 24, 1928, 10; Metcalf & Eddy, "Report to City of San Antonio," 54.

25. *Express*: "Bond Issue For Library," Jan. 17, 1928, 8; "Cut-Off Channel Decision," Jan. 26, 1928, 7; "Channel Width Still Unsettled," Feb. 8, 1928, 10; "Channel Width," Feb. 9, 1928, 9.

26. *Express*: "Channel Width," Feb. 9, 1928, 9; "City Urged To Keep Crecelius," Feb. 14, 1928, 8; "Crecelius Salary Cut," Feb. 28, 1928, 6; "Flood Prevention Office To Close," Aug. 31, 1928, 15; "Crecelius Quits," Sept. 1, 1928, 7; *Light*: "Crecelius Job In Air," Feb. 14, 1928, 1; "Resignation Refused," Feb. 15, 1928, 1.

27. *Express*, "2 Firms Named," Nov. 15, 1928, 10. In a budget-cutting move the next year, the city again consolidated the flood prevention office with the city engineer's office, eliminating twenty-nine of the flood prevention office's thirty employees. (*Express*, "200 Employees," May 26, 1929, 2-A.)

28. *Express*: "City Ready to Call," Aug. 12, 1928, 1-A; "Flood Prevention Work," Oct. 26, 1928, 6;

29. *Evening News*, "River Bed Would Enrich," Feb. 15, 1928, 1.

30. Ibid.; *Light*, "River Land," Feb. 15, 1928, 2-A; *Express*, "Big Bend Not To Be Eliminated," Feb. 16, 1928, 9.

31. *Express*, "'Big Bend' Not To Be Eliminated," Feb. 16, 1928, 9.

32. Ibid.; *Evening News*, "River Bed Would Enrich," Feb. 15, 1928, 1. In recent de-

cades, City Hall has been made the scapegoat for a plan to eliminate the Great Bend. No firm evidence, however, has ever been advanced to support that case, nor has any documentation been offered to further define the women's "counter-movement." No mention of eliminating the Great Bend appears in minutes of city commissioners or the City Federation of Women's Clubs. Although Conservation Society minutes of the time are missing, contemporary histories of the society by its members make no reference to such an effort, as they would have were the uproar as extensive as it was later made out to be. The quick defeat may not have left enough time for the opposition to formalize, leaving those in later days wishing for a quick story having to piece together various conjectures to come up with an explanation, however erroneous, of what happened. (Fisher, *Saving San Antonio*, 210–11.)

33. *Express*: "City Buys," Mar. 16, 1926, 9; "Church Built In 1886," Nov. 5, 1927, 6; "Alamo Widening Project," Dec. 12, 1928, 11. East of the neighborhood, details were being completed in 1928 to widen South Alamo Street. Through southern La Villita, the east-west Nueva Street was already being widened. The tallest building in San Antonio, the new thirty-one-story Smith-Young Tower, rose at the west, where a new bridge across the new cutoff channel would again connect Villita Street with Dwyer Avenue.

34. *Express*: "City Commission Promises," Dec. 12, 1928, 11; "Losoya Extension," Mar. 26, 1929, 22; "Street Will Be Built," Mar. 29, 1929, 28.

35. *Express*: "Street Will Be Built," Mar. 29, 1929, 28; "Losoya Extension Plan," Apr. 14, 1929, 1-A.

36. *Light*, "Losoya River St. Killed!," Apr. 12, 1929, 1; *Express*: "Suspended Street Project 'Ditched,' " Apr. 13, 1929, 24; "Losoya Extension Plan," Apr. 14, 1929, 1-A.

37. *Light*, "Losoya River St. Killed!," Apr. 12, 1929, 1.

38. *Express*, "Losoya Street Extension," Oct. 4, 1929, 1-C.

39. *Express*: "City Given Right," Mar. 10, 1929, 13; "City Will Mark," Apr. 23, 1929, 15. While an 1837 Texas law generally gave the state title to abandoned property along with the ability to sell it, the court ruled that San Antonio maintained title to the riverbed, abandoned or not, under terms of its land grant from the King of Spain in 1730.

40. *Express*: "Famous Old Lawyers' Office Building," Jan. 20, 1927, 6; "River Wall Extended," Apr. 6, 1927, 9; "Home Firm Given," Mar. 20, 1929, 28; "Big Bend Cut-Off Work," Mar. 30, 1929, 22; "Man Fatally Hurt," Oct. 3, 1929, 1. Another landmark in the path of the bypass channel, the 1859 Greek Revival Market House, had already been torn down for the widening of Market Street. Behind the Market House location, the channel took the site of the 1840 Council House Fight between San Antonians and Comanches.

41. *Express*: "Mayor Is Opposed," Oct. 20, 1929, 1-A.

42. Fisher, *Saving San Antonio*, 191; *Express*: "Wider River Channel," Sept. 10, 1929, 7; "Concrete River Channel Doomed," Oct. 22, 1929, 24; "Channel Project Checks," Oct. 23, 1929, 15; "Plans For River Ready," Oct. 26, 1929, 24.

43. *Express*: "Wider River Channel," Sept. 10, 1929, 7.

44. Ibid.

45. Metcalf & Eddy, "Report to the City of San Antonio," 53; *Express*: "City To Condemn Land," Oct. 16, 1928, 28; "Wider River Channel," Sept. 10, 1929, 7.

46. *Express*, "$10,000,000 Buildings," Aug. 12, 1928, 1-C.

47. *Express*: "90-Foot Channel," Aug. 16, 1928, 6; "New Taxable Values," Mar. 30, 1929, 3-C; "12 Acres On River," July 21, 1929, 1-C; Metcalf & Eddy, "Report to City of San Antonio," 61a–62.

48. *Express*: "Mayor To View," Oct. 3, 1929, 10; "Club Women Fight," Oct. 4, 1929, 28; "Women's Clubs to Oppose," Sept. 8, 1929, 1-A; "Wider River Channel," Sept. 10, 1929, 7; "Second Protest," Oct. 5, 1929, 10.

49. *Express*: "City Commission To Decide," Jan. 21, 1930, 26; "Mrs. W.E. Pyne Federation Head," Feb. 21, 1930, 5; *Light*: "S.A. Clubwomen Unite," Sept. 8, 1929, 1; "City Accepts Swiss Plaza," Jan. 27, 1930, 1. This was not the only deal the city made. Pioneer Flour Mills donated a strip of land to widen the channel in exchange for the city's widening of South Alamo Street near its plant and replacing two wooden railroad bridges with steel ones. (*Express*: "City Will Build Bridges," July 27, 1929, 6.)

50. *Express*, "49 Committees Report," May 15, 1928, 10. Six weeks before the convention, the Texas Game, Fish, and Oyster Department's director of natural resources praised San Antonio's compliance with new antipollution laws, saying that the river through San Antonio was "the cleanest in Texas." (*Express*, "San Antonio Praised," Apr. 6, 1928, 4.)

51. *Express*: "Walk To Be Built," Jan. 27, 1928, 9; "Trash Removed," Apr. 4, 1928. The Old Spanish Trail Association was formed to promote paving the old trail from San Diego, California, through San Antonio to St. Augustine, Florida, now the basic route of Interstate 10. Its river committee members, headed by the wife of attorney John L. Browne, included the wives of architect Atlee Ayres and sculptor Gutzon Borglum, plus noted artist Mary Bonner.

52. Fisher, *Saving San Antonio*, 187, 209; *Express*: "River Will Be Lighted," Mar. 25, 1927, 9; "River Lighting Conferences," Jan. 25, 1928, 8; "New River Lights," Feb. 15, 1928, 15; "River Lighting To Be Changed," Mar. 22, 1928, 9; "Flood Lights for Illumination," Mar. 24, 1928, 2; "Monks Lauded," Apr. 5, 1929, 10.

53. Bartholomew, "A Comprehensive City Plan for San Antonio," vii; *Express*: "Mrs. W.E. Pyne Federation Head," Feb. 21, 1930, 5; "City Starts Big Bend Beautification," Apr. 9, 1930, 13.

54. Bartholomew, "A Comprehensive City Plan," 326; *Express*: "River Flow Jazzed Up," Aug. 6, 1927, 4; "Grass on River Banks," Aug. 16, 1928, 3.

55. *Express*, "Artists Advised To Paint River," Apr. 6, 1929, 10.

5. Debating the River Park

1. Zunker, *A Dream Come True*, 3.

2. Garvin, *The American City*, 443; Lovelace, *Harland Bartholomew*, 5; Harland Bartholomew and Associates Collection, http://library/wustl.edu/units/spec/archives/guides/bysubject_stlouis/hba.html.

3. Zunker, *A Dream Come True*, 95.

4. Zunker, *A Dream Come True*, 145; *Express*, "Business Group Looks Ahead," Oct. 30, 1938, 1-A.

5. Ellen Ugoccioni, "The City of Coral Gables: Still an Oasis," *Florida History and the Arts*, Summer 2004, http://dhr.dos.state.fl.us/services/magazine/04summer/article1.cfm;"The History of Coral Gables Venetian Pool," http://www.venetianpool.com/History.html.

6. Cutting a passage through the Book Building is not specifically mentioned in Hugman's writing. His 1929 map of the Shops of Aragon and Romula clearly shows such an entrance, however, and Hugman does refer to a careful wooing of Dwight D. Book, the picturesque building's owner, for support of the river project. (Zunker, *A Dream Come True*, 141.) Later owners of the building cut just such a pass-through to open the rear of the building for riverside patio dining as Hugman had envisioned.

7. The name Aragon has an obvious link with Spain, but Romula appears geographically only as a Roman city in present-day Romania.

8. Fisher, *Saving San Antonio*, 187, 193. The artistic nature of some involved in the evolution of the San Antonio River may have caused their written recollections to combine a sense of dreamy reverie with an annoying lack of precision. In an account Hugman prepared in 1978, he reported that Mrs. Taylor, whom he visited in 1929, was the president of the society, when in fact the president at the time was Margaret Lewis. In the same account, published in Vernon Zunker's *A Dream Come True*, Hugman reports presenting plans to "about 100 prominent people." He begins his next paragraph with the words, "Here are a few names in the '29 era" and proceeds to list seventeen names, most with no identification, without telling whether they received his plans or why they were listed. His next paragraph, inexplicably listing four more names, begins, "Names appearing in the '39 era . . . to mention only a few names at random," a comment as vague and unhelpful as that of what could also have been a more authoritative work, artist Emily Edwards's article on San Antonio Conservation Society involvement with the river, written a few years earlier "just to suggest a continuity of interest." A typescript of Hugman's account, in files of the Conservation Society, appends documentation simply under the heading "Local Newspaper Headlines"—three dozen of them, one third under the heading "1929–1940 Period" and the rest under the slightly more specific "1935–1940 Period." Only three are accompanied by the dates on which they appeared, and none indicates in what newspaper they were published, thus adding further insight into why it has taken so many years to straighten out the saga of the River Walk.

9. C. M. Chambers, "To Whom It May Concern," May 29, 1929. Letter copy in San Antonio Conservation Society library.

10. Fisher, *Saving San Antonio*, 194; *Express*, "Preliminary Steps," June 29, 1929, 8; *Light*, "Unique S.A. Asset," June 30, 1929, pt. 7, 1.

11. Fisher, *Saving San Antonio*, 146; Wilson, *The City Beautiful Movement*, 261, 276.

12. Fisher, *Saving San Antonio*, 134–35; *Express*: "Mayor Names Plan Body," Dec. 7, 1928, 10; "Street Layout In San Antonio," May 26, 1929, 1-A.

13. *Express*, "Prize City Plan Idea," July 16, 1929, 28.

14. Ibid.

15. Ibid.; *Express*, "City Plan Expert," July 19, 1929, 24.

16. *Express*: "Women's Club Members," Oct. 18, 1929, 8; "Landscape Architect To Develop," Oct. 18, 1929, 8; "Landscape Architect Employment," Nov. 16, 1929, 24.

17. Garvin, *The American City*, 443–45. *Express*: "City Planner Views River," Dec. 19, 1929, 26; "Planner Studies River," Dec. 20, 1929, 15; Bartholomew, "A Comprehensive City Plan," 322. Bartholomew served as director of planning for St. Louis from 1916 to 1953 and died in 1989 at the age of 100. Through his work in St. Louis and the influence of the consulting firm he headed for forty-two years, he is credited with institutionalizing the planning function as an integral part of city government.

18. *Express*, "River Boulevard," June 6, 1918, 2-A.

19. Bartholomew, "A Comprehensive City Plan," 279–83, 321–28. Planted along the channel outside the Great Bend, where tall landscaping would slow floodwaters, would be groups of low shrubs, flowers, and vines to climb masonry walls.

20. *Light*, "City Passes Zoning Law," Jan. 27, 1930, 1.

21. *Express*: "Springtime," Mar. 17, 1935, 1-A; "Rock Work Adds," Aug. 4, 1935, 1-A; "Rubiola Backs River," July 10, 1935, 16. In addition, federally funded relief workers were lining 3,000 feet of the river in Brackenridge Park with rock walls.

22. Plans for restoration of Seguin's River Walk have been made by the Walnut Branch Restoration Project, which presents them at www.ci.seguin.tx.us/main-street/wb%20powerpoint.pps.

23. *Express*: "Beautifying River," July 6, 1935, 5; "Rubiola Backs River," July 10, 1935, 16; "Architect Tells of River's Beauty," Oct. 11, 1935, 18; "River Downtown To Be Lighted," Apr. 8, 1936, 16.

24. Fisher, *Saving San Antonio*, 105–6.

25. *Express*, "Dam And Cutoff Control," June 14, 1935, 1.

26. *Express*: "Boats Christened," Apr. 21, 1936, 6; "Venetian Night Attracts," Apr. 22, 1936, 3. White's cochairman in 1936 was Andrew Morales, president of the Mexican Business Men's Association, who brought the boat decoration plans up from Mexico City, presumably from the boats of Xochimilco. Hugman recalled

first being contacted by White after White heard of him at city hall, where White had gone to ask for help cleaning up the river beside the Plaza. (Zunker, *A Dream Come True*, 140.)

27. *Express*, "Not A Gondola In Sight," July 1, 1936, 18. The lifespan of riverside tenants was gleaned from the appropriate San Antonio city directories and telephone books.

6. Creating the River Walk

1. *Express*: "Widely Known Hotel Man," Jan. 23, 1927, 4-D; "Jack White Named Head," Dec. 9, 1948, 1-B.

2. *Express*, "Extensive Beautification," Apr. 24, 1938, 7-A. Other members of the committee were Claude V. Birkhead, Dr. Frederic G. Oppenheimer, L. B. Clegg, L. J. Hart, L. G. Seeligson, Father Rabe, Rev. Walter A. Arnold, Isaac Bledsoe, D. A. Powell, J. H. Turner, J. K. Beretta, and Judge C. A. Goeth.

3. Ibid.

4. Ibid.

5. Ibid.

6. Ibid.

7. *Light*, "City Rejects River Plans," Apr. 28, 1938, 6-B; Improvement District," Sept. 13, 1938, 8-A; *Express*, "Funds Raised," May 22, 1938, 1-C. In mid-1939 the name of the Works Progress Administration was changed to Work Projects Administration.

8. *Express*, "Funds Raised," May 22, 1938, 1-C; *News*, "River Beautification," Aug. 1, 1938.

9. *Express*, "New River Improvement District," Sept. 18, 1938. The city's last previous improvement district, created in 1919, was formed by a neighborhood in the southern part of the city to raise funds to pave its streets, the most common use of the technique. Improvement districts fell out of favor after new legislation permitted the city to charge property owners directly for two-thirds of such costs.

10. *Light*, "Improvement District," Sept. 15, 1938, 8-A.

11. Ibid; *Express*, "Bonds Approved," Oct. 26, 1938, 1. The new improvement entity was officially District No. 15. An intriguing story recounted by Robert Hugman in 1978 has it that only 5 property owners lived in the district, 2 of whom opposed the bonds; that a legal loophole was found to allow votes by Plaza Hotel guests who owned only such personal property as a wristwatch, and thus the favorable bond margin was achieved. (Zunker, *A Dream Come True*, 107.) The story, however, is suspect. Contemporary news reports state that there were 107 eligible voters, and, that while these may have represented only 8 percent of the district's property owners, they owned two-thirds of the district's appraised real property, a percentage valued at $20 million (*Express*, "Bonds Approved," Oct. 26, 1938, 1). It seems unlikely that of as many as 1,300 bona fide riverside property

owners only 5 would own two-thirds of the property value, especially since the 90 businessmen who petitioned for creation of the district were earlier reported as owning property valued at an identical amount (*Light*, "Improvement District," Sept. 15, 1938, 8-A). It may be that some Plaza Hotel guests were found eligible to vote under the loophole, and that a few did so.

12. *News*, "Work On Beautifying," Oct. 26, 1938; *Light*, "River Liason Group," Nov. 10, 1938; *Express*, "Work on River," Nov. 13, 1938. Appointed were White, D. A. Powell, Claude V. Birkhead, Wilbur W. Matthews, Isaac Bledsoe, Dr. Frederic G. Oppenheimer, Walter W. McAllister and Rev. Walter A. Arnold.

13. Maverick's son, Maury Maverick Jr., reported having heard this unattributed story, but could not recall from where. Maury Jr. added that he was told by Louis Lipscomb that the congressman's funding efforts were inspired when Maury Sr. and Lipscomb went down from the street to the banks of the river one night to relieve themselves. Maverick slipped and fell in. "Louis," he said as he pulled himself out, "we've got to do something about this river." (Maury Maverick Jr. to Lewis F. Fisher, interview, Sept. 22, 1996.) The story is sometimes told as having occurred when Maury Sr. was mayor and Lipscomb was his police commissioner, an incorrect time to have inspired funding since by then the river was already funded and the project was well under way.

14. *New York Times*, "Gondolas For Texans," Feb. 12, 1939, 1-XX.

15. *Express*: "E. P. Arneson Funeral," Dec. 8, 1938; "Triple Check," Dec. 16, 1938, 8. Before being executed, plans first had to be approved by the Central Improvement Committee, then by the city council, and finally by the city's flood prevention engineers. Walter Lilly, a consulting engineer, later supervised preparation of San Antonio's second master plan, which he completed in 1951 during the administration of Mayor Jack White. ("San Antonio Master Plan," http://www. salsa.net/aiasa/sa-mastp.html.)

16. *Express*, "Business Group Looks Ahead," Oct. 30, 1938, 1-A.

17. Fisher, *Saving San Antonio*; 193; Work Projects Administration, *Along the San Antonio River*, 22; Zunker, *A Dream Come True*, 148. New stairways to the River Walk were self-supporting and structurally unattached to bridges, preventing separation due to dual actions of vibrations at street level and the movement of water-soaked earth below.

18. Ibid.

19. Ibid.

20. Work Projects Administration, *Along the San Antonio River*, 33; *Light*: "River Project Being Pushed," Apr. 2, 1939, 4-B. Circular boat routes going around the bend, through the cutoff channel, and back into the bend were still impossible, due both to the dryness of the cutoff channel and to its blocking by the flood control dam near the start of the cutoff channel.

21. Work Projects Administration, *Along the San Antonio River*, 12–13, 15. Workmen

removing old channel walls at the southeastern corner of the bend uncovered a nest of freshwater lobsters. (Zunker, *A Dream Come True*, 148.)

22. Hugman to Green, Feb. 1, 1940, letter copy in San Antonio Conservation Society Library.
23. Ibid; Work Projects Administration, *Along the San Antonio River*, 12; Zunker, *A Dream Come True*, 155.
24. Work Projects Administration, *Along the San Antonio River*, 20.
25. Ibid., 22.
26. Ibid.
27. Work Projects Administration, *Along the San Antonio* River, 13, 33; Zunker, *A Dream Come True*, 148.
28. *Express*: "Trees Being Preserved," June 14, 1939, 10; "River Beautification," Mar. 14, 1941, 1-A; Zunker, *A Dream Come True*, 166.
29. Ibid.
30. *Light*, "River Beauty Project," Mar. 29, 1939; *Express*, "Trees Being Preserved," June 14, 1939, 10.
31. Zunker, *A Dream Come True*, 144.
32. Ibid., 114.
33. *Express*: "City To Place," Sept. 17, 1939, 1-A; "Water Fills River," Dec. 24, 1939, 1-A.
34. *Express*, "Trees Being Preserved," June 14, 1939, 10; *Milwaukee Journal*, "Hoosier Vagabond," Dec. 21, 1939.
35. Fisher, *Saving San Antonio*, 196; *Light*: "Rock Work On River Rapped," Dec. 21, 1939, 13-A.
36. Fisher, *Saving San Antonio*, 196.
37. Ayres to Green, Feb. 1, 1940, letter copy in Conservation Society Library.
38. Hugman to Green, Jan. 31, 1940, letter copy in Conservation Society Library.
39. *Express*, "Buenz to Boss River," Mar. 22, 1940, 8.
40. Maverick to Green, Feb. 19, 1940, letter copy in Conservation Society Library.
41. Zunker, *A Dream Come True*, 116.
42. *Light*, "Architect May Fight City," Mar. 22, 1940, 14-A.
43. *Express*, "Buenz to Boss River," Mar. 22, 1940, 8.
44. Fisher, *Saving San Antonio*, 207, 348.
45. *Express*, "River Beautification Project," Mar. 14, 1941, 1-A; Work Projects Administration, *Along the San Antonio River*, 31–32. Hugman designed the maintenance boat so that at night a deck could be drawn over the irrigation gear to form an upper level for musicians cruising the river.
46. Zunker, *A Dream Come True*, 120.
47. Graham, *History of The Texas Cavaliers*, 11, 53; *Express*, "50,000 See Fiesta," Apr. 21, 1941, 1. Member Bill King is credited with the inspiration for Cavaliers sponsorship, and was the group's first river parade chairman.
48. Graham, *History of The Texas Cavaliers*, 53–57; *Express*, "50,000 See Fiesta," Apr.

21, 1941, 1. Fifty of the plywood boats, measuring six by twenty feet, were built by WPA arts and crafts workers on the two lowest floors of the Smith-Young Tower beside the river.
49. *Express*, "50,000 See Fiesta," Apr. 21, 1941, 1. For the parade, Richard Friedrich purchased several paddleboats left from San Francisco's international exposition two years earlier.
50. Graham, *History of The Texas Cavaliers*, 57–58.
51. *Express*, "50,000 See Fiesta," Apr. 21, 1941, 1.

7. Disuse and Rescue

1. Fisher, *Saving San Antonio*, 221–223. The jubilee/festival/carnival typically began as persons descended stairs to nine themed sections, with appropriate foods, costumed workers, and decorated boats anchored along the banks. In early evening, boats headed downstream. Participants followed in a procession along the River Walk to the Arneson River Theater, then formed a mummers' parade on to a Carnival of Nations.
2. Lomax, *San Antonio's River*, 79–80, 81.
3. *Light*, "First New River Boat," Aug. 12, 1945, 6-A.
4. *Light*, "Glamour Out In War Bond Sales," Apr. 19, 1943, 2-A; Lomax, *San Antonio's River*, xxvi.
5. Bill Lyons to Lewis F. Fisher, interview Nov. 27, 1996. At first the restaurant was indoors only. Then an outdoor patio was built at a level higher than the River Walk, since maintenance of a precise water level along the Great Bend was not yet perfected. Then tables beneath umbrellas were added along the River Walk itself. Gas-fed tiki torches added an exotic touch at night along the seldom-used walk across the river from the restaurant. To draw attention from the street, Casa Rio's name was painted on the upper wall facing the river and two torches blazed behind the statue of the Indian on the Commerce Street bridge above.
6. *Express*, "S.A.'s Casa Rio renewed at 46," Oct. 16, 1992, 7-C; *Express Images*, "Keepers of the Flame," Sept. 29, 1996, 4; Zunker, *A Dream Come True*, 150. One source reports the boat concession was being run in 1948 by "the San Antonio River Company, a private concern originally from St. Louis, Missouri." (Lomax, *San Antonio's River*, 83.)
7. Breeding, *Flood of September 1946*, 1, 3, 8. The rainfall beneath the center of the storm was 16 inches, compared with 7 to 8 inches over much of San Antonio.
8. Breeding, *Flood of September 1946*, 8.
9. *Express*, Feb. 23, 1951; *Light*: "Flood Spurred Start," Jan. 1, 1961, 12-A; "Placid S. A. River," Jan. 2, 1961, 29; "Construction Just Beginning," Jan. 3, 1961, 2; San Antonio River Authority, *San Antonio River Authority 1937-1987*, 1, 3, 5, 8. Some work was supervised by the San Antonio River Canal and Conservancy District, predecessor of the San Antonio River Authority and a holdover from the last

grand scheme to straighten and deepen the entire San Antonio River as a barge canal to the Texas coast. The district was chaired by Col. W. B. Tuttle, who had planned the Fiesta river parade in 1907.

10. *Light*, Dec. 13, 1957, 28.

11. Fisher, *Saving San Antonio*, 221, 224, 263. The properties, both limestone block structures built in the mid-nineteenth century, were the Dashiell house at 511 Villita Street and, at the northwest corner of Villita and South Alamo streets, the two-story Bombach building, since 1967 the Little Rhein Steakhouse, set up by Heinie Mueller and sold to Frank Phelps.

12. Fisher, *Saving San Antonio*, 263.

13. "To the Stockholders and Directors of Endowment, Inc.," Nov. 15, 1951, petition copy in San Antonio Conservation Society Library.

14. Fisher, *Saving San Antonio*, 264; *Express*, "City Wins Fight," Oct. 27, 1951; *News*, "Society Loses," June 4, 1952, 22.

15. Holmesly, *HemisFair '68*, 59–60.

16. Ibid., 60.

17. Ibid.

18. *Express*, "River Bend Park," June 1. 1961, 1.

19. Ibid.

20. Ibid.

21. Ibid.

22. Ford to Chamber, May 30, 1961, letter copy in San Antonio Conservation Society Library.

23. Straus to Guerra, Sept. 14, 1992, copy in UTSA Archives, David Straus Papers, Box 5; Ordinance 302382, 1962, copy in UTSA Archives, David Straus Papers, Box 1.

24. Ibid.

25. River Walk Commission Minutes, June 1, 1962, in UTSA Archives, David Straus Papers, Box 2. Other initial members were F. M. Davis of the H. B. Zachry construction company, real estate broker C. W. Fenstermaker, designer Roger Rasbach, Gene Sommerhauser of Lone Star Brewing, insurance executive A. H. Cadwallader, and Straus. Atlee Ayres served on the River Walk Commission until 1967, and remained an active architect until his death two years later at the age of 96.

26. In addition to Wagner and Torres, architects on the committee were O'Neil Ford, Edward Mok, Brooks Martin, Arthur Mathis, Thomas Pressly, and Boone Powell. Allison Peery joined later. Consulting from city government were planner Larry Travis and Bill Hunter, special projects engineer. (River Walk Commission Minutes, Jan. 23, 1963, in UTSA Archives, David Straus Papers, Box 2; Wagner, "Planning for the Development," 5.)

27. Wagner, "Planning for the Development," 3–4; *Express*, "River Bend is Renamed," Apr. 16, 1963, 3-B.

28. Wagner, "Planning for the Development," 4–6.

29. Ibid., 5.

30. George, *O'Neil Ford, Architect*, 158. The project's site, owned by Nick Catalani, was ultimately used for the Hilton Palacio del Rio.

31. Holmesly, *HemisFair '68*, 66–67; *Express*, "Dixieland Night Club," Apr. 4, 1963, 14-F.

32. *Light*, "Restaurant Hailed," June 6, 1964, 7; Holmesly, *HemisFair '68*, 62.

33. *News*, "3 Held in River Assault," Oct. 11, 1962; *Express*, "Police Float Down River Beat, June 24, 1964.

34. Straus to Kubert, June 7, 1962 and Kubert to Straus, June 12, 1962 in UTSA Archives, David Straus Papers, Box 3; Holmesly, *HemisFair '68*, 61. River Square was considered a model for River Walk development. A nondescript building facing North Presa Street was replaced with a brick building one story high at street level and descending to a lower level facing a courtyard with outdoor riverside dining. Overlooking the courtyard at right angles was the rear of a landmark commercial building that fronted on Commerce Street. Its façade was restored, its interior renovated as the Stockman Restaurant, and its back wall pierced with large windows and an entrance to the courtyard. Assisting in the development was Straus's young assistant, Arthur P. "Hap" Veltman Jr., who became a leader in River Walk matters. Veltman opened the long-running Kangaroo Court with Bob Buchanan.

35. David J. Straus to Lewis F. Fisher, interview, June 7, 2006. Straus gave the smaller boat he had built to the Chamber of Commerce.

36. *Express*, "Taxi Contract," Jan. 28, 1967.

37. *Express*, "Downtown HemisFair Site," July 4, 1963, 1. The 350-room El Tropicano Motor Hotel had opened on Lexington Avenue at the northern end of the River Walk in 1962.

38. Fisher, *Saving San Antonio*, 300; *Express*, "All Seven Bond Issues Carry," Jan. 29, 1964, 1. In addition to the new river extension, main River Walk improvements financed included an arched bridge over the entrance to the extension, one behind the Hilton, and a third, designed by the firm of Ayres & Ayres, north of the Commerce Street Bridge.

39. Fisher, *Saving San Antonio*, 313.

40. Zunker, *A Dream Come True*, 156; Fisher, *Saving San Antonio*, 313.

41. Straus to Fisher, June 7, 2006.

42. Huxtable, *New York Times*, "HemisFair, Opening Tomorrow," 49; Black, "San Antonio's Linear Paradise, *AIA Journal*, July 1979, 36.

43. Black, "San Antonio's Linear Paradise," 36.

44. Montgomery, "HemisFair '68," *Architectural Forum*, October 1968, 88. A marina for storing boats and barges was built at the extension's east end. Project archi-

tect was Allison Peery and landscape architect was James Keeter. Engineers were Haggard, Groves and Associates. Contractors were Darragh and Lyda, Inc. and H. A. Lott, Inc.

8. Crown Jewel of Texas

1. As noted in chapter one, the crown jewel reference appeared in a letter to the San Antonio *Express* on Aug. 23, 1887. One "idle dream" remark, mentioned in chapter five, was made in 1929 by Newton H. White, chairman of the San Antonio Chamber of Commerce and head of the City Plan Committee. A 1995 study showed that of the 6.9 million visitors to San Antonio in 1994, the most—82 percent, or 5.6 million—visited the River Walk and 27.5 percent showed the River Walk to be the single most important reason for their visit, more than three times the number listing their top attraction as the city's traditional top sight, the Alamo. (*Express*: "Study says S.A. tourism robust," Oct. 13, 1995, 1.) The River Walk was number one when the Tourism Division of the governor's office began doing surveys in 1998 and kept the spot until 2003, when it dropped behind the Alamo once again. (*Express*, "Alamo strolls past River Walk," Oct. 8, 2004, 1-A.)

2. Sinclair Black, "San Antonio's Linear Paradise," *AIA Journal*, July 1979, 30; *An Evaluation of Expansion Opportunities for the Henry B. Gonzalez Convention Center* (Washington, D.C.: Urban Land Institute, 1995), 8.

3. *Singapore River Development Plan* (Singapore: Urban Redevelopment Authority, 1992), 10; *San Antonio Business Journal*, "Monterrey adding Alamo City touch," Sept. 20, 1996, 1; "Gentrification Moves In," the *New York Times*, Nov. 28, 2005, A-19. A group from Indianapolis returned to lower the White River fourteen feet through the center of its city. Back to Virginia went planners of the $34 million Richmond Riverfront, fifteen feet below street level along abandoned Civil War–era stone-lined canals and locks. "We were incredibly impressed," said the chairman of the Miami River Revival Committee as he returned to Florida to promote a $500 million river project. Others came from Sacramento, Phoenix, Minneapolis, Kansas City, Louisville, Charlotte, Oklahoma City. From Hull, Quebec, came Canadians planning a French village along their new Brewery Creek River Walk. (*Express*, "Richmond likes Riverfront," Dec. 8, 1993, 1-D; *San Antonio Business Journal*, "River Walk now serves as model," Apr. 19, 1996, 14.) In judging the nation's finest walking routes, the American Volkssport Association in 1995 named a two-hour stroll along San Antonio's River Walk as second only to a trail along the Hudson River at West Point.

4. City of San Antonio Ordinance 41341, Oct. 12, 1972, copy in UTSA Archives, David Straus Papers, Box 1.

5. Zunker, *A Dream Come True*, 124. Paul Silber's younger son, John, was a longtime president, then chancellor, of Boston University.

6. Boone Powell to Lewis F. Fisher, interview, Nov. 23, 1996.

7. *Light*, "River Architect Flays Power Barges," Nov. 5, 1972, 17-A; Hugman to Straus, May 30, 1977, letter copy in UTSA Archives, David Straus Papers, Box 1. In 1972, Hugman opposed removing the tainter gate in the cutoff channel so boats could make a circle around the bend, rather than doubling back at each end of the bend, on the grounds that it would stop the natural flow of the river. Nor did he like the idea of a channel from the Alamo to the river, or barges powered by gasoline motors rather than being poled through the water.

8. Six years earlier, in response to a proposal to name various River Walk landmarks after people, Hugman had asked River Walk Commission President Lawrence J. Raba that no such names appear, not even his. Appropriate names could go on a stand-alone historical marker, but otherwise, "all the features are a living part of the living Paseo del Rio—not a graveyard of memories." (Hugman to Raba, Aug. 8, 1972, letter copy in UTSA Archives, David Straus Papers, Box 1.) Nevertheless, in addition to his recreated office sign, Hugman's name was added after his death to the arching bridge he had designed on the northern leg of the bend near what became the Omni La Mansion del Rio.

9. Regnier to Phelps, Nov. 15, 1977, letter copy in UTSA Archives, David Straus Papers, Box 1.

10. The marina houses the main armada of passenger and dining barges, park rangers' patrol boats, and maintenance barges.

11. Hensley-Schmidt, *Olmos Dam Inspection*, 4, 8, 38, 51–52.

12. Carson and McDonald, *A Guide to San Antonio Architecture*, 38; Straus to River Walk Commissioners, Dec. 10, 1986, copy in UTSA Archives, David Straus Papers, Box 1.

13. Lead architect for the Paseo del Alamo, designed by Ford, Powell & Carson, was Boone Powell.

14. *Express*, "Cullum band's radio show," May 9, 2004, 1-J.

15. *Express*, "Down by the river," May 12, 2001, 1-E. The first noise control regulations, implemented after two years of study, included banning amplified band music mostly after 10 p.m. Sundays to Thursdays and after 11 p.m. Fridays and Saturdays. As new clubs drew crowds of younger San Antonians to mix with more restrained tourists, regulations were tightened six years later. A long-running debate of how independently the River Walk should be overseen intensified in 1992, when the city combined the River Walk Commission with the Fine Arts Commission and the Historic Review Board to create the Historic Design and Review Board, dealing with citywide issues as well as the River Walk.

16. *Express*, "Elite greenery," July 22, 2004, 1-A. Eight years earlier the American Society of Civil Engineers had named the River Walk a National Historic Civil Engineering Landmark.

17. *Express*, "Lady Eco to speed up," June 23, 2006, 1-B. Funding was contributed by the private San Antonio Parks Foundation, headed by River Oversight Committee cochair and former mayor Lila Cockrell. Implementation was under the

direction of River Operations Supervisor Lincoln St. George.

18. "Downtown Renaissance Looks to Retail 'Eden' on the Riverwalk," *Texas Architect*, Sept.-Oct. 1988, 9; "Just add water," *Architectural Record*, March 1989, 100. The mall, which created 3,000 jobs, was attracted through the efforts of Mayor Henry Cisneros and City Manager Tom Huebner and first planned in 1980 by national developer Edward J. DeBartolo Corp. and Allied Stores. Restaurants were at river level, with most retail outlets at street level and above. Behind the mall was a parking garage for 3,100 cars. The mall was designed by Urban Design Group and Communications Arts of Tulsa, and work involving water was designed by San Antonio's Ford, Powell & Carson. The Marriott Rivercenter was designed by Baltimore's RTKL.

19. Fisher, *Saving San Antonio*, 491.

20. *Express*, "Center of Attention," Nov. 25, 2001, 1-H. Lead architects for the project were Steve Tillotson and John Kell of Kell Munōz Architects plus Ken Fowler of the landscape architecture firm Rialto Studios.

21. The scope of events overseen by the Paseo del Rio Association, many of them with corporate sponsorships, is indicated by the schedule for 2006: Jan. 12–15: Michelob Ultra River Walk Mud Festival, during draining of the river for maintenance, incorporating a Mud Pie Ball, Pub Crawl, Mud Coronation, Mud Parade, and Arts and Crafts Show; Feb. 24–26: Mardi Gras Arts and Crafts Show; Feb. 26: Bud Light Mardi Gras River Parade; Mar. 17–19: Dyeing O' the River Green and St. Patrick's Day Parade; Apr. 22: Harcourt Children's Festival; Apr. 25–28: Ford Mariachi Festival, middle and high school mariachi bands on barges; May 25–26: Memorial Day Arts and Crafts Show; June 30–July 3: July 4th Arts and Crafts Show; Aug. 19: Ford Canoe Challenge, ninety canoe teams competing; Sept. 1–4: Labor Day Arts & Crafts Show; Sept. 14: Dos Equis Pachanga Del Rio, a culinary sampling on the River Walk extension from twenty River Walk restaurants; Oct. 6–8: Fall Arts and Crafts Show; Nov. 24: Ford Holiday River Parade and Lighting Ceremony. Arts and crafts shows are held along the broad sidewalk areas of the River Walk extension.

22. *Express*: "Let there be Lights," Nov. 29, 1996, 1-C; "The Light Stuff," Nov. 29, 2002, 1-B.

23. Fisher, *Rosita's Bridge*, 32. Rosita's father and two uncles were WPA workers on the River Walk and its bridges.

24. Fisher, *Saving San Antonio*, 439; *Express*, "A work in progress," July 5, 2001, 1-B. The San Antonio Conservation Society contributed $150,000 to help match a federal Economic Development Administration grant for building the arches.

25. The largest new hotels included the Holiday Inn Riverwalk (325 rooms, built in 1987); Adam's Mark/Crowne Plaza (410 rooms, 1997 in the former National Bank of Commerce Building); the Westin Riverwalk (513 rooms, 2002), on the Great Bend's southern leg by the Mill Bridge; the Valencia (265 rooms, 2003), on Houston Street at the river; Patrick Kennedy's luxury Watermark Hotel and Spa (99 rooms, 2004), across the bend's northern leg from his La Mansion del Rio, both purchased by Omni in 2006; the Contessa (265 rooms, 2005), by the Mill Bridge across from the Westin; and Drury Plaza Hotel (310 rooms, 2006), in the former Alamo National Bank Building near the east side of the cutoff channel. A 34-story, 1,000-room Hyatt was due to open in 2008 beside the northeast corner of the Convention Center.

26. *Express*, "River Walk clamp on chains eyed," Apr. 16, 2006, 1-A.

27. Ibid; *Express*, "Ousted owners lament," Jan. 10, 2006, 1-E.

28. *Express*, "Battle for the River Walk," Mar. 12, 2006, 1-K.

29. *Express*, "River Walk clamp on chains eyed," Apr. 16, 2006, 1-A.

30. *Express*: "S. A. sues 4 River Walk firms," Apr. 2, 1998, 1-A; "River Walk dispute settled," Aug. 14, 2001, 1-B.

31. Ibid.

32. *Express*: "O'Malley barge group sinks rival," Mar. 10, 1995, 1; "Awash in years of change," Nov. 21, 2004, 1-B. In 1998 an independent company sought to operate its own boats on the river, but courts decided that the San Antonio River was not a public waterway under federal law and that the City of San Antonio could limit barge traffic in the interest of public safety. (*Express*, "Brothers run aground," July 14, 1998, 1-B.)

33. *Express*, "Flood could have been even worse," Oct. 25, 1998.

34. *Express*, "Recycled water begins flowing," June 20, 2000, 8-B.

35. *Express*: "River upgrade gets under way," Jan. 31, 2001, 8-B; "Revamped river," Mar. 19, 2002, 1-B; "Changes true to spirit," Apr. 7, 2002, 1-H. Landscape architect for the project was Bender Wells Clark Design. Punched-metal light fixtures were designed by Judith Maxwell.

36. *Express*, "Weston Centre plans," Mar. 18, 2005, 1-D.

37. *Express*: "New park links," Oct. 1, 2001, 3-B; "River link evolves," Oct. 14, 2001, 1-H.

38. *Express*, "River Walk link," Oct. 21, 2004, 1-B.

39. "Currents and Eddies," http://www.sanantonioriver.org/pdfs/Currents_and_Eddies_May8_red.pdf. Sidewalks, art works, and other amenities are to follow a city-commissioned master plan by Seattle's Lorna Jordan Studio in association with San Antonio's Bender Wells Clark Design.

40. "San Antonio River Improvements Project,"http://www.sanantonioriver.org/overview.html; "An Old River's Revival," http://www.c-b.com/information%20center.The project's master plan was being coordinated under San Antonio River Authority Director of Watershed Management Steve Graham. Architect for the Museum Reach is San Antonio's Ford, Powell & Carson and architect for the Mission Reach is the San Antonio office of Carter & Burgess.

41. "An Old River's Revival," http://www.c-b.com/information%20center.

42. *Express*, "River project to turn back clock," Jan. 8, 2004, 8-B.

Baker, T. Lindsay. *Building the Lone Star.* College Station: Texas A&M University Press, 1986.

Bartholomew, Harland, and Associates. *A Comprehensive City Plan for San Antonio.* St. Louis, 1933.

Bartlett, C. Terrell. "The Flood of September, 1921, at San Antonio, Texas." *Transactions of the American Society of Civil Engineers* 85 (1922): 354–77.

Booth, John A., David R. Johnson, and Richard J. Harris, eds. *The Politics of San Antonio: Community, Progress and Power.* Lincoln and London: University of Nebraska Press, 1983.

Black, Sinclair. "San Antonio's Linear Paradise." *AIA Journal* (July 1979): 30–38.

Breeding, Seth D. *Flood of September 1946 at San Antonio, Tex.* Geological Survey Circular 32. Washington: United States Department of the Interior, Nov. 1948.

Burkhalter, Lois W., painted by Caroline Shelton. *San Antonio: The Wayward River.* San Antonio: Trinity University Press for Paseo del Rio Association, 1979.

Bushick, Frank. *Glamorous Days in Old San Antonio.* San Antonio: The Naylor Company, 1934.

"Canoeing on the San Antonio River," *San Antonio: The Passing Show* 1, no. 37 (July 27, 1907): 4–5.

Carson, Chris, and William McDonald. *A Guide to San Antonio Architecture.* San Antonio: San Antonio Chapter of the American Institute of Architects, 1986.

Coppini, Pompeo. *From Dawn to Sunset.* San Antonio: The Naylor Company, 1949.

Corner, William. *San Antonio de Bexar.* San Antonio: Bainbridge & Corner, 1890.

Cox, I. Waynne. *The Spanish Acequias of San Antonio.* San Antonio: Maverick Publishing Company, 2005.

Ellsworth. C. E. *The Floods in Central Texas in September 1921.* Geological Survey Water-Supply Paper 488. Washington: Department of the Interior, 1923.

Everett, Donald E. *San Antonio: The Flavor of Its Past, 1845–1898.* San Antonio: Trinity University Press, 1975.

Everett, Richard. "Things In and About San Antonio." *Frank Leslie's Illustrated Newspaper* VII, no. 163 (Jan. 15, 1859): 95–96, 102–3.

Ewing, Thomas E. "Waters Sweet and Sulphurous: The First Artesian Wells in San Antonio." *Bulletin of the South Texas Geological Society* 60, no. 6 (Feb. 2000): 9–22.

Fisher, Lewis F. *Crown Jewel of Texas: The Story of San Antonio's River.* San Antonio: Maverick Publishing Company, 1996.

_____. *C. H. Guenther & Son at 150 Years: The Legacy of a Texas Milling Pioneer.* San Antonio: Maverick Publishing Company, 2001.

_____. *Saving San Antonio: The Precarious Preservation of a Heritage.* Lubbock: Texas Tech University Press, 1996.

Fisher, Mary McMillan. *Rosita's Bridge.* San Antonio: Maverick Publishing Company, 2001.

Fox, Ann A., Lois M. Flynn and I. Waynne Cox. *Archaeological Studies for the San Antonio Channel Improvement Project, Including Investigations at Guenther's Upper Mill (41BX342).* Report No. 136. San Antonio:

University of Texas at San Antonio Center for Archeological Research, 1987.

Frary, I. T. "The River of San Antonio." *Architectural Record* 45 (Apr. 1919): 380–81.

Garvin, Alexander. *The American City.* New York: McGraw-Hill, 1996.

George, Mary Carolyn Hollers. *O'Neil Ford, Architect.* College Station: Texas A&M University Press, 1992.

Graham, Henry. *History of the Texas Cavaliers, 1926–1976.* San Antonio: Texas Cavaliers, 1976.

Guerra, Mary Ann Noonan. *The San Antonio River.* San Antonio: The Alamo Press, 1987.

Gunn, Clare A., David J. Reed and Robert E. Couch. *Cultural Benefits From Metropolitan River Recreation—San Antonio Prototype.* Technical Report No. 43. College Station: Texas Water Resources Institute, Texas A&M University, June 1972.

Hensley-Schmidt, Inc. *Olmos Dam Inspection For City of San Antonio, Texas.* Chattanooga, 1974.

Holmesly, Sterlin. *HemisFair '68 and the Transformation of San Antonio.* San Antonio: Maverick Publishing Company, 2003.

Hugman, Robert H. H. River Walk architectural drawings (prints). San Antonio Conservation Society Library.

Huxtable, Ada Louise. "HemisFair, Opening Tomorrow, Isn't Texas-Size, But It's Fun." New York Times, Apr. 5, 1968, 49.

Industries of San Antonio, Texas, The. San Antonio: Land & Thompson, 1885.

Knight, Larry. "Defining American in San Antonio in the 1850s." *Southwestern Historical Quarterly* CIX, no. 3 (Jan. 2006): 319–35.

Lomax, Louise. *San Antonio's River*. San Antonio: The Naylor Company, 1948.

Lovelace, Eldridge. *Harland Bartholomew: His Contributions to American Urban Planning*. Urbana: University of Illinois Dept. of Urban and Regional Planning, 1993.

McDowell, Catherine. "San Antonio's Mills on the River," 1974, ms. in San Antonio Conservation Society Library.

McLean, Bert J. *The Romance of San Antonio's Water Supply and Distribution*. San Antonio: San Antonio Printing Co., 1927.

Metcalf & Eddy. *Report to City of San Antonio, Texas, Upon Flood Prevention*. Boston, 1920.

Montgomery, Roger. "HemisFair '68, Prologue To Renewal." *Architectural Forum* (Oct. 1968): 88.

Morrison, Andrew. *The City of San Antonio*. St. Louis: George W. Englehardt and Company, 1889.

Newcomb, Pearson. *The Alamo City*. San Antonio: Standard Printing Company Press, 1926.

Olmsted, Frederick Law. *A Journey Through Texas*. New York: Dix, Edwards & Co., 1857.

Phelps, Christi. "Shading the Future," *San Antonio Monthly Magazine*, Jan. 1987: 112.

Ramsdell, Charles. *San Antonio: A Historical and Pictorial Guide*. Austin: University of Texas Press, 1959.

[San Antonio Chamber of Commerce.] *San Antonio*. San Antonio: [San Antonio Chamber of Commerce, 1915].

San Antonio City Commissioners Minutes, 1915–30. City Clerk's office, San Antonio.

San Antonio, City of, and San Antonio River Authority. *Conceptual Plan for the San Antonio River from Nueva Street to U.S. Highway 281*. San Antonio, 1993.

San Antonio *Express*.

San Antonio *Light*.

San Antonio River Authority. *San Antonio River Authority, 1937–1987*. San Antonio, 1988.

"San Antonio, Texas." *Berlin Bridges and Buildings*, Berlin Bridge Co., East Berlin, Conn. 1, no. 9 (Dec. 1898): 126–28.

Santleben, August. *A Texas Pioneer*. I. D. Affleck, ed. New York: Neale Publishing Company, 1910.

Sibley, Marilyn McAdams. *George W. Brackenridge, Maverick Philanthropist*. Austin and London: University of Texas Press, 1973.

Skidmore, Owings & Merrill, Marshall Kaplan, Gans, and Kahn. *San Antonio River Corridor*. San Francisco, 1973.

"Soldiers and the Flood." *The Trail, Published in the Interest of the Second Division*, Camp Travis, Tex. 1, no. 37 (Sept. 16, 1921): 1–15.

Spofford, Harriet Prescott. "San Antonio de Bexar." *Harper's New Monthly Magazine*, Nov. 1877: 831–50.

Steadman, Doug. "A History of W. E. Simpson Company from 1909 to 1993." San Antonio, 1993.

Steinfeldt, Cecelia. *Art for History's Sake: The Texas Collection of the Witte Museum*. San Antonio: The Texas State Historical Association for the Witte Museum, 1993.

_____. *San Antonio Was: Seen Through a Magic Lantern*. San Antonio: San Antonio Museum Association, 1978.

Stothert, Karen E. *The Archaeology and Early History of the Head of the San Antonio River*. Southern Texas Archaeological Association Special Publication No. Five, Incarnate Word College Archaeology Series No. Three. San Antonio: Southern Texas Archaeological Association in cooperation with Incarnate Word College, 1989.

Straus, David J. Papers. University of Texas at San Antonio Library Archives.

Wilson, William H. *The City Beautiful Movement*. Baltimore and London: Johns Hopkins University Press, 1989.

Work Projects Administration Writer's Program in the State of Texas, comp. *Along the San Antonio River*. American Guide Series. San Antonio: City of San Antonio, 1941.

Zunker, Vernon G. *A Dream Come True: Robert Hugman and San Antonio's River Walk*, rev. ed. San Antonio: N.p., 1994.

INDEX